A PHILOSΟ

D0726102

ON PHILOSΟ

Most books on philosophy are unintelligible to most intelligent people. On a rough estimate over half of what passes for philosophy is unreadable.

ON PHILOSOPHERS

The philosopher is just as likely to swear as anybody else when he breaks a shoe-lace or misses a train, and he is no better able to conceal his irritation when he steps on a nail, or his pain when he bites his tongue.

ON THE VALUE OF PHILOSOPHY

The general teaching of the great tradition of philosophy is that, if we live as we ought, we shall know things as they are, and that if we see things as they are, our vision will help us to live as we ought. This is not merely a creed for the learned. It is a faith which many simple folk have embraced. Thus philosophy provides men less with a faith by which to live than a scale of values to regulate their living. These values can serve not only as ideals to guide the individual's life, but as ends to direct the actions of all mankind.

PHILOSOPHY

by C. E. M. Joad

A PREMIER BOOK

FAWCETT PUBLICATIONS, INC., GREENWICH, CONN.

MEMBER OF AMERICAN BOOK PUBLISHERS COUNCIL, INC.

A Premier Book published by arrangement with English Universities Press, Ltd.

Second Premier printing, October 1965

Premier Books are published by Fawcett World Library,
67 West 44th Street, New York, N. Y. 10036
Printed in the United States of America

CONTENTS

CONTENTS

CONTENTS

Chapter 1

ON READING PHILOSOPHY

The Difficulty of Philosophy

PHILOSOPHY is an exceedingly difficult subject and most books on philosophy are unintelligible to most intelligent people. This is partly, but not wholly, due to the difficulty of the subject-matter, which, being the universe, is not surprisingly complex and obscure. There is no reason, at least I know of none, why the universe should necessarily be intelligible to the mind of a twentieth-century human being, and I take leave to remind him how late a comer he is upon the cosmic scene and how recently he has begun to think.

I cannot resist the temptation, thus early in the book, to introduce a time-scale to enforce the point. It is estimated that there has been life of some sort upon this planet for some 1,200 million years; [1] human life for about a million. Human civilization, giving the most generous interpretation to the term "civilization", has endured for about two and a half thousand years. Now, the period during which it is estimated that the heat of the sun will be sufficient to support the conditions necessary to life, as we know life, is about 1,200,000,000,000 (twelve hundred thousand million) years, or about a thousand times as long as the whole past history of life.

Let us scale these figures down to make them manageable. If we put the past of life at one hundred years, then the past human life works out at about a month and of human civilization at about 1¾ hours. On the same time-scale, the future of civilization—that is to say, the future during which it may be supposed that man will continue to think—is about one hundred thousand years. It was about

[1] The estimate is of course only approximate. It may be hundreds of millions of years out; some would estimate the duration of life upon the earth as nearer six hundred or even three hundred million years.

two thousand five hundred years ago, between 600 and 400 B.C., that the human mind seems for the first time to have turned over in its sleep, shaken itself and looked about it. Even then it was in the minds only of a few very exceptional individuals that this increase of awareness, which we call thinking, took place. Confucius, Buddha, Lao Tse and Socrates were all born during these two hundred years; Plato and Aristotle followed within the next hundred. But these were exceptional individuals, biological "sports" on the intellectual and spiritual plane, pointing the way forward to a level of human development to which the race as a whole may one day advance. (It must be confessed that it has shown little disposition to do so during the two thousand three hundred years that have elapsed since this initial leap.)

By any reckoning, then, the human mind is very young, and it is not to be expected that it should, as yet, understand very much of the world in which it finds itself. Indeed, there is a sense in which the more we know, the more we become aware of the extent of our ignorance. Suppose, for example, that we think of knowledge as a little lighted patch, the area of the known, set in a sea of environing darkness, the limitless area of the unknown. Then, the more we enlarge the area of the lighted patch, the area of the known, the more also we enlarge the area of contact with the environing darkness of the unknown. In philosophy, then, as in daily life, cocksureness is a function of ignorance and dunces step in where sages fear to tread. The wise man is he who realizes his limitations, a truth to which the famous legend of Socrates prompted by the oracle at Delphi to go on his unsuccessful search for somebody wiser than himself, bears witness.[1]

The Difficulty of Philosophers

The subject-matter of philosophy is, then, necessarily obscure, and this obscurity philosophy necessarily reflects and expresses. But besides the expression of obscurity there is also obscurity of expression, and, while the former is pardonable, the latter is not, being, when all is said and done, nothing but bad craftsmanship. The object of words is to express meaning, and he who has learnt to use them well,

[1] You can read it—it is worth reading—in the Dialogue of Plato known as *The Apology*.

will express his meaning with the greatest ease and clarity. Hence, a writer should make it his first duty to be clear and intelligible, not only in justice to himself, but also out of compliment to his readers. Few philosophers have observed this elementary rule.

"But the figural synthesis, when it is considered merely in relation to the original synthetic unity of apperception, that is, to the transcendental unity which is thought in the categories, must be called, in distinction from the purely intellectual combination, the transcendental synthesis of imagination."

That is from Kant. Some of the terms employed are technical, and some acquaintance with the special senses in which they are used is necessary to a full understanding of the meaning of the passage. Also it is fair to point out that Kant wrote in German and that the sentence I have quoted is, therefore, a translation. But when all allowance is made for these facts, Kant is still intolerably and unnecessarily obscure; so much so, that volumes have been written by his commentators and critics with the object of determining not whether what he said was true, but what he meant by what he said. Much of this trouble would have been saved, if Kant himself had taken more pains with his writing.

Here is another example which is modern, which is not a translation and in which there are no technical terms, from Professor Whitehead's *Science and the Modern World*:

"The aboriginal data in terms of which the pattern weaves itself are the aspects of shapes, of sense-objects, and of other external objects whose self-identity is not dependent on the flux of things. Wherever such objects have ingression into the general flux, they interpret events, each to the other. They are here in the perceiver; but, as perceived by him, they convey for him something of the total flux which is beyond himself. The subject-object relation takes its origin in the double rôle of these eternal objects. They are modifications of the subject, but only in their character of conveying aspects of other subjects in the community of the universe."

Professor Whitehead is, in the opinion of many, the most

eminent contemporary philosopher and *Science and the Modern World* is, by any reckoning, a great book. Yet it is continuously marred by Professor Whitehead's inability or unwillingness to take the pains which are necessary to express himself clearly.

Partly because of the necessary obscurity of the matter expounded, partly because of the unnecessary obscurity of its expositors, much philosophy is difficult to the point of unintelligibility. On a rough estimate over half of what passes for philosophy is unreadable.

On Reading Philosophy

It follows that the first caution to be given to those who are proposing to tackle philosophy is at all times to approach the original philosophers with the greatest circumspection, and not at any time to try to read them without guidance. Guidance can best be given by a lecturer or tutor at a University, who should make it his business to tell you what to select for your reading. It is even more imortant that he should tell you what to skip. Nearly all books on philosophy are too long and, provided that one masters the key passages, all but these can be safely ignored. Thus, the good teacher will say, "You might read Chapter I, pages 1-17, of Bradley's *The Principles of Logic* on the General Nature of Judgment, but for goodness sake don't go on beyond that until we have had an opportunity of discussing it, so that I can see how much of it you understand."

But suppose that you have nobody to say these things to you, and no opportunity of discussion. Then it is desirable that you should lay down certain rules for your reading and do your best to follow them.

First, never try, at any rate in the beginning, to read the whole of a book on philosophy. Pick out certain chapters—two or three, perhaps—which deal with matters that seem to you to be of particular importance or which relate to topics on which you have already read something and which you wish to follow up, and concentrate on these. For example, you may be interested in the problem of causation. Very well, then, you take up Hume's *A Treatise of Human Nature,* read the first four Sections of Part III and for the time being neglect the rest. The first rule, then, is judicious selection.

Judicious selection involves a preliminary inspection of

Chapter headings and the intelligent use of the index, in order to find out where the topics that most interest you are to be found; it also entails the reading of the Introduction or Preface, whether written by the philosopher himself or by the modern writer who introduces him, so that having obtained a preliminary bird's-eye view of the territory which you are about to enter, you may the more easily find your way, avoiding the deserts and spotting the oases.

Secondly, even within the areas selected, you will find difficult and boring passages which you will do well to omit. The author, you will find, repeats himself; skip the repetitions; he is, you will also find, from time to time unintelligible; omit the unintelligible paragraphs, even if you return to them for a second try later on. The second rule, then, is intelligent skipping.

Thirdly, take care never to go on reading unless you are understanding—the word "understanding" being interpreted in a generous sense—what you read. This injunction sounds obvious, yet such is the difficulty of philosophy that many readers habitually fail to observe it. I have known students to read themselves into a state of limp discouragement by dint of simply pegging away out of sheer doggedness, sheer stupidity or both, at something that they didn't understand and had better have left alone. As a result they were effectively "put off" philosophy for the rest of their lives. Keep, then, a careful watch upon yourself to make sure that you are understanding what you read and drop the passage abruptly and go on to something else, if you are not.

Fourthly, in order to make sure that you *are* understanding, take careful notes, making your own *précis* of the passage you are reading, so that, when you want to refresh your memory, it is to the *précis* you turn, your *précis,* and not to the original. It is also useful to make a private index of the various points that have struck you in the course of your reading as being of outstanding importance or interest on the two or three blank pages which publishers thoughtfully provide for the purpose at the ends of books.

All this means that to read philosophy, as it should be read, is to engage in an active process in which all the faculties of the mind are working at full stretch. For the process is as various as it is active and involves a number of different tasks. There is the task of finding out precisely what the

writer means by what he says; the task of considering what
its bearing is upon the meaning of what he has said before,
of determining, in other words, its general relevance to the
argument as a whole; there is the task of considering what
you personally think of it, of deciding, that is to say, whether
to reject it or to try to incorporate it into the structure of
your own thought, and, if you decide to incorporate, the
task of fitting it into the framework of your own ideas. This
may involve modifications both in the new ideas to be received and in the existing framework into which they must
be fitted, these latter modifications being frequently arduous
to the point of acute mental discomfort, involving, as they
do, a re-arrangement of mental furniture and sometimes the
jettisoning of a number of familiar and valued antiques. This
last is a task from which we increasingly shrink as we grow
older and after middle-age are usually unable to perform
at all.

Finally, there is the task of determining to the best of
your ability whether what you are reading is true, and this
requires a degree of concentrated absorption which few
people can compass for more than a short period. Hence—
another rule—never read philosophy for more than half or,
at most, three-quarters of an hour at a time. At the end of
that period your concentration will begin to slacken, your
attention to flag, until, bored and dispirited, you throw the
book aside and proceed to turn to your novel with such a
nasty taste in your intellectual mouth that it is only by a
considerable effort of will that you will ever be able to take
up your philosophy again. As the transition from thoughtful
and interested attention to the beginnings of inattention is
difficult to mark, be always on the look-out for it, so that,
detecting it in its early stages, you will be content to put
your philosophy down while you are still ready to go on
with it. Success in the study of philosophy, like success in
eating, in drinking, in games-playing, in working, in friendship, even in love-making, depends upon one's willingness to
stop while one has both the energy and the desire to continue. Prepared to taste any drink once, we should never
drink any to the dregs.

Parenthetically, with what an added gusto one turns to
the reading of literature after a spell of philosophy. How
easy, how restful the novel appears, like free-wheeling down

a hill after a grinding climb up the slope; also, how full of the color and richness of humanity.

The Value of Philosophy

I had intended to stop here, but my teachers told me that I ought not to end a chapter with a parenthesis—though, for the life of me, I cannot see why I should not. I have been taught to give heed to my teachers and so I propose to add a word on the value of philosophy. It is, so far as I can see, non-existent. Philosophy, that is to say, will not help you to acquire fame or wealth, to win promotion at the office, to commend yourself to eminent persons, or to be a nicer or more agreeable person. It will not endow you with a distinctive disposition, or equip you with that desirable attitude to life known popularly as the philosophic temperament by virtue of which you are enabled to bear the toothaches and pimples of experience with more equanimity than the nonphilosopher.[1] The philosopher is just as likely to swear as anybody else when he breaks a shoe-lace or misses a train, and he is no better able to conceal his irritation when he steps on a nail, or his pain when he bites his tongue.

Philosophers are no more noticeably successful at managing their lives than other men. Unlike astrology, Spiritualism, Christian Science, psychoanalysis, and other contemporary aspirins for the sick headache of mankind, philosophy provides its students with no esoteric information on how to control the self or predict the future. No world-famous philosopher tells you how to make friends, acquire influence over others, or overcome your inferiority complex. Philosophy, again, offers no protection from impending danger, does not cure loneliness, allay fear or provide a sanatorium wherein the spirit of man may find a refuge from the increasing chaos of the contemporary world.

Why, then, study philosophy? It is difficult to read and hard to understand; its subject-matter is obscure and its professors write obscurely about it; to be read to advantage it demands the assistance of a tutor and opportunities for discussion, and it is apparently of no practical value what-

---

[1] But see Chapter 7, pp. 179–182, for some qualifications, though, in spite of the advice on p. 13, you are bidden not to read them until you get to Chapter 7.

soever. No honors reward the efforts of the philosopher, no employer is in need of his qualifications, nor does philosophy equip him to make his way in the world. Why, then, study philosophy?

There is only one answer to the question. To satisfy the impulse of curiosity. Some of us want to know the meaning of this surprising world in which we find ourselves, to understand the significance and, if possible, to discover the purpose of human life in general and of our own lives in particular. What is the point of life and how ought it to be lived? Philosophy concerns itself with these questions, not aspiring to answer them with finality, but considering and discussing them and studying the answers which have seemed convincing to greater men than ourselves. Philosophy, then, is a record of the soul's adventures in the cosmos. Some find enjoyment in the pursuit of mental and spiritual adventure; these are philosophers, and only those who share their tastes are advised to set foot upon the trail which they have blazed.

Chapter 2

SUBJECT-MATTER AND SCOPE

In this chapter I propose to try to answer the question, "What is philosophy about?" and, incidentally, to substantiate the somewhat grandiose claims made for it at the end of the last, as the record of the soul's adventures in the universe.

Philosophy is, I think, most appropriately to be conceived as a clearing house to which the results of all other human inquiries are brought and in which the records of all forms of human experience are sifted, assessed and evaluated.

The Reports from the Sciences

Consider, for example, the sciences. Physics gives us information about the ultimate constituents of matter as revealed by contemporary analysis. These constituents are, it seems, not solid; indeed, they lack all the familiar properties of the objects of the common sense world. Their movements are not always in accordance with discoverable laws, while their behavior is analogous sometimes to that of waves, sometimes to that of projectiles. If they are to be pictured at all, they may most appropriately be conceived after the model of electrical charges which are, nevertheless, not charges *in* anything. But if we ask what is their real nature, physics does not tell us; it only gives us information about their behavior.

Chemistry investigates the laws of the combination of these ultimate constituents of matter, establishes formulæ for the composition of elements, tells us how many elements there are and explores their relations to each other. Carrying its researches into more highly organized forms of matter, it describes the combining of elements to make molecules and of molecules to make compounds.

Biology gives us information about a particular class of highly organized chemical compounds which exhibit the property known as being alive. How, if at all, it asks, do these organic compounds, as they are called, differ from so-called inanimate matter? How many forms of life are there? How does one form pass into another, and what are the laws which determine whether a particular form will survive and develop or die out; and what, incidentally, does "development" mean? All these are questions with which biology concerns itself. Branching off from biology, there is the science of genetics, which gives information about the laws of inheritance and asks what precisely it is that the offspring receives from its parents at conception. If, as seems to be the case, its inheritance consists of packets of chemicals called genes, can we say anything about the laws which will determine what genes it will receive, and how they will determine its characteristics?

Anthropology takes for its subject-matter a special subsection of the creatures that are living—namely, those that are called human beings—describes their forms of behavior and social grouping, seeks to discover the emotions by which they are swayed and the beliefs which they entertain. It shows how early groupings develop into more complex ones. Sociology asks the same questions and seeks the same information in regard to those more complex and recent forms of human grouping which we call civilized societies.

Physiology and anatomy describe the contents and seek to elucidate the laws determining the workings of the human body. Psychology, albeit with marked lack of success, seeks to describe the constituents and workings of the human mind or, as some psychologists prefer to say, of the living organism considered as a whole.

Each science working within its own sphere obtains its own set of results. But it is not the business of any one of the sciences to co-ordinate its results with those reached by the others, with a view to drawing up a map of the whole territory each department of which has been separately investigated. It is as if each science were entrusted with the cultivation of a separate set of trees, but it was nobody's business to concern himself with the wood. Inevitably, then, no scientist sees the wood; he is too preoccupied with his allotted trees.

The Philosopher takes the Field

It is here that the philosopher steps in. His concern is

with the wood; the wood, that is to say, considered as a whole. He gathers together and collates the results of the sciences, not with a view to querying them—he accepts them; how indeed could he do otherwise, since he has not the qualifications either to reach the results himself or to check those reached by others?—but with a view to assessing their meaning and significance. He is like a commander sitting in his tent some distance away from the battle in continuous receipt of reports from his generals who are in the thick of the fight, from which he must try to piece together a picture of the battle as a whole. He, if anybody, is in a position to tell how it is going and what the outcome is likely to be.

Here, for example, says the philosopher, is the report of the physicists which seems to show—or used to; there have been modifications recently—that the only things that exist are bits of matter moving about in space. But here again is the biologist speaking of something that he calls "life". Some of the biologists seem to think that life can be shown to be a by-product of matter, subject to the same laws as those which, according to the physicists, determine the workings of matter. This does not, on the face of it, seem very plausible (though in saying this, I am afraid that I, the author, am intruding my own views) but, if it is not plausible, does it not follow that there are at least two different principles in the universe, life and matter? If there are, how do they interact?

Here, again, is the report of the psychologists who treat of something called "mind" or "consciousness". This sets a new problem, for how does "mind" fit into the scheme? Is it simply a particular form of life, life as it were at a higher level, but owning the same origin and constituted of the same essence as the life of the amoeba, or is it the expression or creation of the mind of a superhuman personality? Or is it, perhaps, just a mode of the brain's functioning, or a by-product of the brain? It is with these and similar questions that the philosopher greets the scientists' reports.

The Reports from History, the Arts, Morals and Religion

But the sciences are not his only sources of information; there are all the varied forms of human experience. There is the experience of the ordinary man as he goes about the familiar everyday world, being born, growing up, falling in love, struggling, seeing visions, growing old and dying; there is history, the record of humanity's adventure on this planet. Is history, asks the philosopher, merely a succession of chance happenings, civilizations rising and falling without rhyme or reason, or does it bear witness to the working out of a law, even perhaps to the fulfilment of a plan? If so, can we divine that plan and assist its development, and, if we can, should we try to do so? And what sort of a plan is it?

There is the experience of beauty. What is the source of the mysterious hold that art has upon us and what the significance of works of art? Is beauty just the name which we give to that which we happen to appreciate, a kind of highbrow confectionery? Or is it perhaps a window through which men may glimpse a different world owning a different order of reality? A similar question arises in regard to morals. Every thing and every creature in the world except man acts as it must, or acts as it pleases; man alone acts on occasion as he ought. Whence, then, arises this mysterious pull of duty in virtue of which we are enabled sometimes to oppose and overcome inclination; whence the obligation to do the right? And what incidentally do we mean by "right"? Merely that which makes in the long run for happiness, or a principle rooted in the nature of things, part of the fundamental structure of the universe? If the latter, is the universe fundamentally a moral universe, and is its order, in spite of all the apparent evidence to the contrary, a moral order? If there *is* a moral order in the universe, some mind, one would suppose, must have planned it. Is the universe, then, the creation of a mind? And with these questions we come to the most perplexing and important evidence of all—the evidence from religion.

As we look back over the history of man, we cannot but notice that in all ages many have felt the need of God, sought to see the universe as the outcome of His plan and to discover their part in its working out. Some men, whom we call saints and mystics, have even claimed direct experience of God. But suppose, the philosopher reflects, that the claim is fictitious and that God and beauty and goodness and right and truth are not principles inherent in a reality outside and independent of ourselves, but figments created by our own needs, the need to find comfort in our loneliness, to invest our insignificance with importance and to seek the fulfilment of our aspirations, figments which we proceed to project on to the empty canvas of a meaningless universe.

The Questions for Philosophy

Reports on all these matters are sent in to the philosopher; they are personal reports, often conflicting reports, and they evoke the kind of question of which I have given examples. From these reports the philosopher must try to make a coherent survey of this puzzling universe in which we live, a survey which must include a treatment of—it can scarcely aspire to include an answer to—the time-honored questions which in all ages men have asked about the universe. Has it, for example, point and purpose, or is it merely a fortuitous concourse of atoms? Is mind fundamental in the scheme of things, or is it a by-product of material substances at a particular point of their development? Or is matter itself an illusion born of our limited vision? Are right and wrong, beauty and ugliness, principles existing in their own right independently of ourselves, or are they high-sounding names with which we seek to dignify our human preferences and aversions? Is the world of objects spread out in space the only world, or is there another world, conceivably spiritual and owning a higher degree of reality than the familiar world? Are time and space, change and substance, features of the world outside us, or merely the forms under which we are compelled to conceive it, blinkers as it were, which limit and, it may be, distort our vision?

It is with these questions that the philosopher concerns himself, and to assist his consideration of them he draws upon every field of human experience and holds all the sciences in fee. Facts, it is true, he must know, but he is concerned not so much with the facts as with their meaning; not so much with conclusions as with their significance. His, it is obvious, is an editor's job, and the paper which he must endeavor to bring out is the journal of the universe. As a good editor, he cannot help but recognize that every happening has importance, nor is he entitled to reject anything out of hand as irrelevant.

The Generality of Philosophy

Philosophy, then, is the most general of all forms of

human inquiry. All is grist to the philosopher's mill, ethics as well as science, logic as well as religion, history as well as art. From this point of view, philosophy may be described as the study which is without restrictions upon its subject-matter. Every other branch of human inquiry limits its own scope. Consider, again, in this connection, the sciences. Physics, the most general of the sciences, is concerned with matter as such; its nature, its analysis and the laws which govern its movements. Chemistry is concerned with matter at a certain level of organization; it studies matter under the forms of the element, the molecule, and the compound. Biology makes a further restriction; it concerns itself only with matter that is animated by life; in other words, it studies living organisms which consume food and use it to repair and build up the fabric of their bodies. Botany takes for its sphere those living organisms which absorb water and carbon dioxide from the air and mineral salts from the soil, and by virtue of the chlorophyll contained in their cells transform into living tissue the radiant energy of sunlight—in other words, it is concerned with vegetable life. The scope of zoology is restricted to those living organisms which take in proteins from without, transform it into the tissues of their own bodies and reproduce their kind (these definitions are, of course, incomplete; they may even be inaccurate, nor can they be made complete and accurate without more knowledge than I possess); of anthropology, to that species of living organism which is called man. Psychology restricts itself to those organisms which possess mind or, as it is sometimes called, consciousness.

I have cited the sciences, but similar restrictions apply to other branches of inquiry. History takes for its subject-matter the past of mankind upon the earth; music, the creation and reproduction of patterns of sound; theology, the nature and purposes of God. Philosophy alone is interested in everything that exists simply because it exists, without restrictions of any kind. It studies, as Aristotle puts it, "the nature of being as such".

The Branches of Philosophy: (1) Metaphysics

But philosophy itself has branches. The branch of philosophy which conforms most closely to Aristotle's description and which is, therefore, the most fundamental, is known as metaphysics. What, it asks, is meant by saying of a thing that it exists? Are there certain characterstics which are common to all forms of existent? If so, what are they and what can we know about them? Are there different ways of existing? Philosophers, in their rôle of metaphysicians, have given many different answers to these questions. Some have felt that the familiar world of facts upon which our senses feed is in some sense unreal; it is, they have maintained, only an appearance of a reality which underlies it. If we take it as real—as existing that is to say in its own right—we quickly find ourselves enmeshed in contradictions. Many philosophers have set themselves to examine the features of the familiar world—time, space, change, substance, or the law of cause and effect—and have sought to reveal the contradictions to which the examination gives rise. The human mind, they have demonstrated, when it attempts to understand these familiar features, reaches an antinomy.[1] An antinomy is a pair of conclusions each of which seems to be inescapably true, but which are such that, if one is true, then the other conclusion cannot be true. (The opposition between determinism and free will constitutes a familiar example of an antinomy.) Now, reality, it is said, cannot be irrational; it must make sense. Hence the conclusion is drawn that these features of the familiar world cannot be wholly real.

This is the line taken by some well-known metaphysicians in the nineteenth century who belonged to the school known as Objective Idealism, of which Hegel in Germany and Bradley in England were leading exponents. Reality, they insisted, is a unity; a unity of thought according to Hegel, of experience or feeling according to Bradley, which expresses itself in all the diversity of minds, persons and apparently inanimate things which constitute the everyday world. If reality is a unity—is, that is to say, one—it follows that the apparent differences between things are not in the last resort real; if reality is thought, it follows that matter is illusory.[2]

A similar distinction between reality and appearance was made by Plato, though for different reasons. Reality, for him, consisted of a community of Forms, Truth, for example, and Justice and Beauty and also squareness, whiteness and

---

[1] I give one or two examples of this mode of treatment in a later chapter (see Chapter 4, pp. 89–96).

[2] See Chapter 4, pp. 87–89, for a brief account of this view.

softness, which are neither mental nor material, but are the originals or archetypes upon which our world is modelled. Some account of Plato's views will be given in the next chapter.[1] Reality, Leibniz maintained, is a colony of souls, which he called monads. Reality, according to Berkeley, consists of ideas in the mind of God. Both these philosophers were known as idealists because they affirmed that only mental existents, such as ideas, are real and that matter is illusory; indeed, most metaphysicians have embraced idealism in one or other of its many forms. Descartes maintained the independent reality both of mind and of matter, and bequeathed to his successors the apparently insoluble problem of explaining their interaction.

These are only some of the answers which metaphysicians have given to the question, what is the nature of the things that exist, or, to repeat Aristotle's phrase, of "being as such"? More specifically, they are answers to the question, what is the nature of the reality that underlies the familiar world?

The Categories or Classes of Existents

A rather different question is, what are the different forms which reality assumes, or, alternatively, into what classes, or categories, can "being" be divided? What, in other words, are the fundamental kinds or classes of the things that exist?

I will cite two illustrative answers to this question, one from Greek, the other from contemporary thought. Aristotle answers the question by making a distinction between subjects and predicates. There are some things, which he calls subjects, of which, he says, other things are predicable but which are not themselves predicable of anything; there is another class of things which can be predicated of other things but *of* which nothing is predicable. To the first class we may assign as examples the species horse or the species man. They are examples of the ultimate kinds or types which, according to Aristotle, we find in nature; to it also belong this particular table, this individual horse and John Smith. Of all these we can predicate qualities and attributes; of the first that it is square, of the second that it is frisky, of the third that he is a bank clerk earning $4500 a year. We can predicate these same qualities and attributes, squareness, friskiness and "being

[1] See Chapter 3, pp. 43–46.

a bank clerk", of other individuals and things; but of attributes and predicates, of squareness and friskiness and "being a bank clerk", we cannot predicate anything. Thus, while subjects require nothing else for their existence, attributes and qualities require something else—namely, subjects—in order that they may exist. Here then, in the division between subjects and predicates is one division between existents. It is the class of subjects, or rather the sub-class of this class defined by Aristotle as "neither predicable of a subject, nor present in a subject"—for example, this particular horse or this individual man—which he regarded as substances "in the truest and most primary sense of the word", as being, in other words, the things of which the universe consists.

This division of Aristotle's has given rise to the philosophical problem of substance. It has been extensively discussed and criticized and other divisions on similar and different lines have been suggested. A contemporary division of existents suggested by Professor Whitehead postulates four classes, namely:

> "(1) The true and real things which endure,
> (2) The true and real things which occur,
> (3) The abstract things which recur,
> (4) The Laws of Nature.

An example of the first heading is a piece of rock, or—to pass beyond mere physical science—the individuality of a human being, his soul. An example of the second kind is any happenings, in a street, in a room, in an animal body, or—again to pass beyond mere physical science— our individual complex experience within a tenth of a second. An example of the third type is the shape of a rock. It seems doubtful whether a shade of color, or the qualitative element in the performance of a musical symphony, are to be reckoned as concerned with nature or mentality. But certainly they recur." (In other words, the same shades, the same kind of goodness or badness of harmony or dissonance can characterize different objects and different performances.) "On the other hand," Dr. Whitehead continues, "a *sort* of feeling of affection is a recurrence which belongs decidedly to the mental side of things. An example of the fourth heading is the Law of Gravitation, or the geometrical Relations of Things."

(2) Theory of Knowledge

A further branch of philosophy is known as theory of knowledge. This may be distinguished from metaphysics as follows. Hitherto we have written as if the universe is, as it were, laid out for investigation by the inquiring mind of the philosopher which, with certain inconsiderable and recognizable exceptions, knows it exactly as it is. We have made, in other words, the common sense assumption that the function of mind in knowing is broadly that of a searchlight, lighting up a world which exists independently of it and disclosing it exactly as it is. A process of philosophical [1] analysis shows that there is little ground for this assumption. For example, if the assumption is true, what account are we to give of error? Can the searchlight light up what is not there? Presumably not. The mind, then, when it falls into error presumably makes mistakes in the sense that it falsely reports what is there, or even invents what is not there. But, if the mind can invent what is not there, manufacturing the objects which it believes itself to know, how are we to set limits to its inventive capacity? How distinguish the occasions on which it is knowing what exists independently of its own knowing activity from those on which it is creating its own objects of knowledge by its activity?

Reasons were advanced by the philosopher Kant for supposing that the mind always introduces a contribution of its own into the structure of the world that is, as it were, initially given to it to know, even if its contribution is limited to providing a set of pigeon-holes to which the raw stuff that comes to it from without is assigned and in which it is arranged and labelled. Again, there are plausible reasons for supposing that at least some of the things I know are events occurring in me, are, that is to say, psychological happenings in my own mind or physiological happenings in my own body. For example, if I stick a pin in my finger, both the act of feeling and the pain which I feel—that is to say, both the knowing and what is known—are events happening in me. Similarly, if, being color blind, I see as gray something which a person of normal vision sees as green, it is difficult to

[1] Examples will be found in Chapter 4, pp. 72–89.

avoid the conclusion that the color of the thing seen is, at least in my case, dependent upon the peculiar characteristics of my visual apparatus. The color, in short, would seem to be contributed by me; but if this is true of the gray color that I see, it is difficult to suppose that it is not also true of the green color that the person of normal vision sees. Hence arises the suggestion that color is not a quality of things but is contributed by, or is at least dependent upon, the mind of the person who sees them; that it is, as the philosophers Berkeley and Locke put it, an idea in the mind. This mode of reasoning can be extended to show that all the qualities of the so-called external world are dependent upon or, as it is sometimes put, are *in* the mind of the perceiver.[1]

From considerations of this kind there arises an inquiry concerning the general nature of knowledge. Does the process that we call knowing ever introduce us to a world which is wholly external to and independent of ourselves? If some part at least of what we know is dependent upon, or contributed by us, can we tell which part, and is it always the same part? Are there any laws which determine the nature and extent of our mental contributions to the objects which we know, laws which would enable us to say that, when the "contributing" takes place in accordance with them, we shall have what is called valid knowledge; when it takes place otherwise than in accordance with them, invalid knowledge? Again, the question may be raised, are there limits to our knowledge? Even if we suppose that there are certain things which we can know exactly or approximately as they are, may it not be the case that there are some categories or kinds of existent that we cannot know, simply because our minds are not fitted to comprehend them? For example, God, or the nature of free will, or immortality?

Historically, these questions were introduced into philosophy as the result of a discussion of the origins or sources of our knowledge. Does all our knowledge, philosophers asked, originally come to us through the experiences of our sense organs, or is the mind fitted with certain principles or faculties which operate, as it were, independently of sense experience, so that if the mind reasons validly in accordance with them, they will provide it with knowledge of the nature of things which owes nothing to experience? For example, when we reach conclusions by doing sums in mental arith-

[1] See Chapter 4, pp. 76–78; 87–89.

metic, it would not seem *prima facie* that the knowledge we obtain is derived from any one of our five senses.

(3) Ethics, (4) Aesthetics and (5) Politics

There are three subsidiary branches of philosophy which, most philosophers would agree, cannot be fruitfully pursued without reference back to metaphysics and theory of knowledge.

(3) Ethical Philosophy

First, there is ethical philosophy. Ethics, which occupies an important position in the history of philosophy, investigates the nature of good and right or, as philosophers put it, "the good" and "the right". Are these, it asks, independent principles rooted in the nature of things which the mind recognizes, ends or ideals after which the spirit of man strives? Or are they merely names with which we dignify our personal feelings (or the community's feelings) of approval and disapproval? What do we mean by saying of an action that it is right—that it has certain desirable consequences, for example, that it promotes the greatest happiness of the greatest number of people, or that it secures the approval of an intuitive, moral faculty which is innate in the human mind? What is the sanction of duty? Why, that is to say, should we ever do what we know that we ought to do, as opposed to what we want to do?

It is easy to see how these problems impinge upon theory of knowledge and metaphysics. You may hold, as Kant did, that our minds are not, so far as their intellectual faculties are concerned, fitted to know reality, since, whenever they try to know it, they insensibly alter it, "cooking" it, as it were, in the process; but you may also hold that we have other faculties, through which we obtain direct access to reality, precisely because in respect of our possession of these faculties we are ourselves members of the real world. In Kant's view, the will, in so far as it is exercised morally—in so far, that is to say, as it prescribes our duty and commands its performance—is such a faculty. When we recognize the pull of duty, when we *will* to act as we ought, then, he held, we are functioning as members of the real world—the world, that is to say, as it *really* is, as opposed to the world which appears to our senses and is known by our intellects.[1]

Again, you may hold that reality contains a number of eternal principles which can be dimly apprehended by the human mind and which in some sense form the true objects of human knowledge and the goals of human aspiration and effort. The judgment of mankind throughout the ages has usually identified these principles with Truth, Goodness, and Beauty. Hence, in knowing what is good, in feeling and obeying the obligation to do what is right, we are responding to the pull of certain fundamental features in the real world, which are often called "Values" or "the Values".

(4) Aesthetics and (5) Political Philosophy

Similar questions arise in regard to aesthetics. What, philosophers have asked, do we mean by saying of a picture that it is beautiful? Is beauty a principle existing independently of us, or is it simply a projection on to the canvas of an aesthetically neutral universe of our own feelings of appreciation and admiration? If we conclude that it is an independent principle, a factor in the fundamental make-up of things, what deductions are we entitled to draw in regard to the nature of a universe that contains beauty as an independent principle? What, moreover, is the relation of the principle of beauty to the works of art that embody it?

Political philosophy raises, in regard to the community, questions analogous to those which ethics raises in regard to the individual. What, it asks, is the origin of society and what is its purpose? By what principles is society held together? What is the basis of political obedience? What are the comparative merits of various forms of governments, and what is the best form of government? What should be the relation of the individual to his community? Does the individual possess rights which the community is bound to respect? If so, whence do they derive?

The Subjective Factor in Philosophy

From this brief glance at the main departments of philosophy, it will be seen how far-reaching is the territory which it seeks to cover. No mind, it is obvious, can cover all of it,

[1] See Chapter 5, pp. 125-127.

and even of the area which he selects for treatment the philosopher can take only a bird's-eye view.

From this necessary limitation of purview arises a new difficulty. The philosopher selects his sphere of operations; he further selects the topics with which in that sphere he proposes to deal. On what principle does he select them? He selects, it is obvious, what he considers to be of interest or importance. But "interest" and "importance" are subjective factors—are, that is to say, personal factors. What interests me may be without significance to you; what one age thinks important another may deem trivial. For example, in the nineteenth century men's minds were exercised over such problems as Baptismal Regeneration and Prevenient Grace; in the Middle Ages they canvassed the existence of essences, such as "fieriness" or "stoniness"; today few know the meaning of the former problems, or feel more than a derisive interest in the latter. It is obvious, further, that the philosopher's interests, tastes and temperament will determine in some measure not only the topics he selects for study, but the way in which he treats them. So, too, will the age in which he lives. In the Middle Ages the problems with which philosopers concerned themselves were largely set for them by theology, and they sought to make their conclusions square with the teachings of the Christian revelation. Today it is by science, rather than by theology that the philosopher is provided with his material, as he seeks to assess the significance and expose the limitations of the physicist's account of the universe.

If subjective factors determine the topics a philosopher selects and the mode of their treatment, they also influence his conclusions. Philosophy, as I pointed out above,[1] is concerned less with facts than with their meaning and significance. But meaning is what *a person* finds in something; significance what *a person* attributes to it. One man, for example, will see in the universe purpose and design, where another will perceive only a chaos of uncorrelated facts; one man will account for phenomena mechanistically—that is to say, in terms of their causation by preceding phenomena—while another interprets them teleologically—that is to say, in terms of the end at which they may be conceived to be aiming, or the purposes which they are designed to serve. For this reason, every philosophy is bound to give us a

[1] See p. 18–19.

certain amount of information about the philosopher who propounds it. We should be thankful if it succeeds in giving us information about anything else. I say this, not because I do not myself believe that philosophy has succeeded in providing us with information about the nature of things, but because there are many who deny that it has or *can* have any but a subjective reference. It is important, they say, as psychology is important—in the sense that it tells us what certain human beings have *thought* about the universe—but it has no importance as what the film producers call "documentary"; it does not, that is to say, tell us anything about the universe. What, according to these critics, the philosopher is doing and all that he is doing is to project as creator the ideas and wishes of the human mind on to the stage of a meaningless universe, and then to hail as discoverer the characters whom he himself has invented in a play which he himself has written.

This view is, I think, mistaken, for it can, it is obvious, be turned against itself. If the view were true, it would only succeed in telling us something about the minds of those who put it forward; it would not say anything about the matters to which it purports to relate. It would not, that is to say, succeed in referring to the subject which it is proposing to discuss—namely, the extent to which philosophy can tell us about something other than the philosopher; it would only tell us something about the minds of those who hold that particular philosophical view. In other words, if philosophy is only a reflection of the mind of the philosopher, the view that it is so, since it purports itself to be a philosophical view, instead of referring to philosophy, will only reflect the mind of the person who holds it.

But it is not necessary to go all the way with this philosophical nihilism to concede that every philosophy must be, at least in part, a personal document. The point is put with admirable force by Professor Whitehead in describing the work of an eighteenth-century historian. The volumes of Gibbon, he writes, "are at once a detailed history of the Roman Empire, and a demonstration of the general ideas of the silver age of the modern European Renaissance. This silver age, like its Roman counterpart seventeen hundred years earlier, was oblivious of its own imminent destruction by the impact of the age of Steam and of Democracy, the counterparts of the Barbarians and of the Christians. Thus, Gibbon narrates the Decline and Fall of the Roman Empire and exemplifies the prelude to the Decline and Fall of his own type of culture."

It should scarcely be necessary to make the related point that the impact of a philosophy upon the reader will be no less personal than the imprint of its author's mind. Some philosophies, to put it colloquially, are one's "cup of tea", others are not. Whether they will be congenial or not, depends no doubt in part upon the demands of one's intellect; but it depends scarcely less upon the idiosyncrasies of one's temperament. Among the many divisions of mankind into different classes and types, few are more fruitful than William James's distinction between "tough" and "tender" types of mind. It is a distinction which interprets the conclusions of men's intellects, and which therefore represents their philosophies, as the by-products of their temperaments. Some men are "tough", some "tender" in disposition, and as a consequence some will be disposed to accept "tough", others "tender" philosophies. Tough-minded men are "empiricist, sensationalistic, materialistic, pessimistic, irreligious, fatalistic, pluralistic, sceptical". Tender-minded are "rationalistic, intellectualistic, idealistic, optimistic, religious, free-willist, monistic and dogmatical".[1]

For myself, I confess to a general toughness of intellectual undertone shot through with occasional unrepresentative streaks of intellectual tenderness; which means, of course, that I am naturally disposed to give attention and respect to some philosophies rather than to others—and to do this irrespective of their intrinsic merits. Every reader will, if he is honest, admit to a similar tendency.

Now these intellectual preferences and aversions of ours seem to bear little relation to truth. More precisely, some men start with an instinctive predisposition to think true what others will think false and *vice versa*. These predispositions are the result of our inherited make-up and bear a close relation to our wishes. But though wishes may father thoughts, they do not breed evidence.

Difficulty of Philosophy

I hope that I have said enough to show that philosophy is difficult and why it is difficult. It is difficult:

[1] The meaning of some of these terms, in so far as they are technical, will appear in later pages.

(1) because of the scope of its subject-matter and of its obscurity;

(2) because of the unnecessary obscurity of philosophers;

(3) because of the subjective factor which, entering into all philosophizing, makes it hard to distinguish statements which give information about the universe from those which give information merely about the philosopher;

(4) because of the subjective factor which enters into the attitude of the reader, who approaches philosophy not as a formula in algebra which is just true or false, but as a picture of the universe which is living or lifeless, satisfactory or repellent, and finding it to be one or the other accepts or rejects it less because of the intrinsic merits or demerits of the picture, its verisimilitude or lack of it, than because of the disposition, the temperament, the hopes and the wishes which he brings to its consideration.

Variety of Philosophy

From what has been said it will also be deduced that philosophies are very various in their nature. Some embrace the universe in their scope; they purport to tell us about the nature of everything. Others confine themselves to a number of carefully delimited problems, as, for example, to the nature of judgment—what, they have asked, is the nature of the mental operations involved and what is the logical status of our judgment when, for example, we judge wrongly that it will rain tomorrow?—the nature of relations—when we say that a cushion is under the table, what, philosophers have asked, is the precise status of the relation denoted by the word "under" and what is its relation to the table and to the cushion?—or of the object of perception—is it, they have asked, physical, a sense datum, for example, a patch of color, a rap of sound or a felt surface, or is it a sensation occurring in the mind of the philosopher?

The manner of philosophies is as various as their matter. Some philosophies, written in the high metaphysical manner, exhibit formidable chains of deductive reasoning unhampered by distracting references to empirical fact. Bradley's *Appearance and Reality* is a famous philosophical work of this kind; another, in our own age, is Alexander's *Space, Time and Deity;* another, Whitehead's *Process and Reality*.

In recent years, however, this method of philosophizing has tended to go out of fashion and in treatises which have no more color than a mathematical text-book philosophers classify types of propositions and discuss the correct analysis of the meaning of sentences. Much early philosophy—this is particularly true of philosophies which come from the East— consists of inspired sayings and aphorisms which in Hindu philosophy are called Sutras, and of commentaries upon them. Chinese philosophy often takes the form of anecdotes and fables with a philosophical moral; the celebrated Tao-Te-King distils wisdom and preaches detachment. Some philosophies, again mainly Eastern in origin, claim to interpret a hidden wisdom discernible only to those who have subjected themselves to a certain discipline of life, and proceed in the light of this wisdom to prescribe a code of conduct for men. The nature of reality being so-and-so, this, the illuminated philosopher has said, is the way in which men ought to live.

Plato proceeded by the method of dialogue, the characters in Plato's dialogues having spoken parts not unlike those of actors in a play. The dialogue form is a highly serviceable instrument for the exposition of philosophical ideas. A theory is announced by one character; objections to it are put into the mouth of another; the objections are developed by a third, countered by a fourth and answered by the first, while an agreed summary of the discussion may be formulated by any one of the speakers.

Of Aristotle's philosophy, we have for the most part only lecture notes taken by his students between the gaps in which it is often possible to read different meanings. Mediaeval philosophy is, as I have already mentioned, written for the most part with a definite end in view—namely, that of reconciling the theories of Plato and/or Aristotle with the doctrines of Christianity, with the result that the themes with which it is concerned wear a remote air today. The development of science was not without its effect upon philosophy and with the advent of the seventeenth century we find philosophers devoting their attention to problems of perception. What, they asked, do we actually observe of the external world? How much of what we think we observe exists independently of us? With the eighteenth and nineteenth centuries philosophy grows increasingly obscure, while by the twentieth it has attained the condition which I described at the beginning of the first chapter when I remarked that most philosophy is unintelligible to most intelligent people.

Some Qualifications of the Ideal Philosopher

Finally, it will, I hope, have become clear that the student of philosophy needs a considerable educational equipment. In the first place, he should know Latin and Greek, in order that he may read the classical philosophers and understand the Latin tags and Greek allusions that are scattered up and down the works of most philosophers. He must know something of the history of human societies, especially when he is studying the problems of political philosophy; for the full understanding of political philosophy he also needs a knowledge of law. The ethical philosopher must have some acquaintance with theological systems and also with the history of men's moral notions; these requisites entail some knowledge of theology and of anthropology.

When engaged in reading metaphysics and theory of knowledge, the philosopher will need a working acquaintance with science, at least to the extent of being cognizant of the theories of the ultimate nature of physical matter which are fashionable at the moment and of *some* of the evidence on which they are founded. Of the sciences, physics, biology and psychology are specially relevant to the pursuit of philosophy; physics, since it is the most advanced of the sciences and has reached a point at which the researches of physicists increasingly, though regrettably, take them into the territory of philosophers—many books by contemporary physicists seem unable to conclude without one or two chapters on philosophy, in which most of the mistakes which philosophers have themselves made in the past and subsequently exposed will be found crowded within the compass of a score of pages; biology, because of the continually recurring controversy as to whether the behavior of living organisms can be wholly accounted for by the laws of physics and chemistry or whether it requires for its interpretation the introduction of some non-material and purposive principle which is not subject to mechanical causation; psychology, because the investigation by scientific methods of the nature and workings of the human mind would, if only it were attended by agreed results, throw light upon some at least of the problems which interest philosophers, for example, the problem of perception, the relation of the mind to the body and the sources and limitations of our knowledge. (Psychology, by the way, took its rise from within the bosom of philosophy, but has grown impatient of the apron-strings which still tie it to its parent, and aspires to be a separate science in its own right.)

Above all, the philosopher should have some acquaintance with and, if possible, appreciation of literature, music and painting. He must know what great men have thought and said memorably about life, and he must be sensitive to beauty in some at least of the forms of its manifestation, that he may be in a better position to assess its significance and to give some account of the mysterious phenomenon we call genius and of the scarcely less mysterious process known as inspiration, which he must somehow seek to fit coherently into his scheme of the universe.

The would-be philosopher as I have pictured him is, it is obvious, the impossible possessor of impossible knowledge. No man can hope for such attainments nor, though ideally desirable in one who aspires to understand the nature of the universe as a whole, are they practically necessary. Nevertheless, it is true that people should not tackle philosophy unless they are in the commonly accepted sense of the term "well educated". "You must get educated before you do philosophy", I am moved to exclaim half a dozen times a term to University students who, ignorant alike of science and history, of literature and Latin, are forced by their resolve to pursue philosophy to try, comparatively late in life, to grapple with these ancillary studies which they should have mastered in boyhood. Philosophy, then, should be the climax of the ladder of education, not its rungs.

I hope that nothing in the foregoing will lead the reader to believe that I consider myself to possess the knowledge which I have prescribed. Such a belief would be illusory. I know little history and less science; I rarely read poetry, which I find difficult to understand, and have never studied logic. More important than these deficiencies is the fact that I am a parochial philosopher whose mind is anchored in the thought of Europe, and of the philosophy of the East I have only a journalist's smattering. Much of it, and more particularly

Indian philosophy with its vague profundities and inexpressible truths which it will insist on seeking to express, is alien to me. I have been brought up on Greek philosophy and have a fair working knowledge of Plato and of Aristotle, but Mediaeval philosophy is, for me, a comparative blank and, so far as the moderns are concerned, I have found myself too often bogged in their obscurities to be able to lay claim to the knowledge which a scholar and a teacher should ideally possess. Kant and Hegel in particular I find almost impossible to read. I am parochial, too, in respect of my partiality for the English philosophers.

Description of the Book

These being my limitations, I cannot do other than impose them upon my readers. I must assume, that is to say, that they take no more kindly to the more difficult philosophers than I do myself, and shall recommend for reading and for discussion only those philosophers who have succeeded in expressing themselves with comparative clarity. For treatment I have chosen only those topics about which I feel able to write clearly myself.

The result is a highly selective book devoted to specially selected topics which are, I hope, neither unrepresentative nor unimportant.

I propose to begin with Plato and to devote the next chapter to an account of some of the ideas of what I take to be the greatest single book written on philosophy—possibly on any other subject—Plato's *Republic*. Plato's *Republic* is popularly regarded as a sketch of a Utopia, and it is true that it contains an account of the formation and constitution of what Plato calls an ideal State. It also seeks to describe the good life for man. It deals, then, with political and ethical philosophy. But both the ethical and political pictures are presented within the frame of a general conception of the universe as a whole. They flout many of our modern preconceptions and, taken out of their frame, are apt to seem arbitrary and repellent to those of us who have been nurtured in the atmosphere of democracy. I propose, then, to reverse the usual order of treatment and to describe first the metaphysical foundation, and, secondly, the ethical and political proposals which are based upon it. In later chapters I shall say something about the problem of perception and some of the leading ideas of ethical and political philosophy.

Chapter 3

PLATO'S PHILOSOPHY

The Relativity of Sense Qualities

PLATO'S metaphysical theory takes its starting-point from an examination of the objects of the familiar world. These, at first sight, seem solid and durable; but this appearance vanishes under closer scrutiny. The ordinary conception of such a familiar object as, say, a chair or a desk represents it as a substance possessing a number of qualities. The substance is, for example, hard, square, brown, wooden and so on. But do these qualities subsist in their own right, as fixed and definite characteristics of the desk, or is it not rather because of their relation to other things that we say they are qualities of the desk? Plato answers that they only seem to be what they are relatively to a particular point of reference. Choose a different point of reference and you will find that they turn into their opposites. A rabbit, for example, is of a certain size. Is it a small size or a large one? We can only answer that it is small relatively to an elephant, large relatively to an earwig. Here is water of a certain temperature; is it hot or cold? The answer is that it is neither, or rather, that it is both; hot to a man who has come out of a blizzard, cold to one who has just emerged from the stokehole of a steamer. Here is a picture by Landseer; is it beautiful or ugly? It was thought beautiful in the nineteenth century; it is pronounced practically worthless in the twentieth. Whatever quality we like to choose shows an equal tendency to turn into its opposite. In other words, a thing can be said no more truly to possess it than it can be said to possess its contrary quality. As Plato puts it, a thing fluctuates and oscillates between two qualities, or rather between the two poles of the same quality. It is both small and large, hot and cold, beautiful and commonplace; it also has whatever quality there may be between these pairs of opposites. Plato concludes that it cannot properly be said to possess in its own right any fixed and definite quality.

Now, most of the statements that we are in a position to make about a thing take the form of specifying either its qualities or its relations to other things. Thus the desk, we said, is hard, square, brown and wooden. It is related to the floor by being "on" the floor, and to the chair by being twice as heavy as the chair. It also possesses a certain "value", determined by reference to what it costs to buy, which, in its turn, involves a relation to other things which are bought with money. These other things will share in the disabilities of the desk, in that their qualities, too, will turn out to be relative. Plato concludes, first, that no definite statement which is absolutely true can be made about the qualities of the desk, and, secondly, that none of these qualities can be certainly and absolutely known, since in order that a thing may be an object of certain knowledge, it must be fixed and stable and possess fixed and stable qualities. The qualities of the desk, then, are not objects of certain knowledge.

The Elusiveness of Substance

But what of the desk itself, the substance, whatever it may be, that *has* the qualities? This turns out to be surprisingly elusive. It is, we suppose, something that has the qualities, something to which they belong, something which is, nevertheless, other than they. If we were to take the qualities away, it is the substance, we should naturally conclude, which would be left. Let us make the experiment. First, we will take away the hardness. We are left with something that is square, wooden and brown; next the squareness, and we are left with something that is wooden and brown; next the woodenness, and there is left a brown something. Now let us take away the brownness; what remains? Something presumably that had these qualities but has them no longer. Can we say anything about this "something"? Apparently not, since, as we have seen, any statement we make about a thing is couched in terms of its qualities and relations, so that if we were sufficiently thorough in our stripping away of the qualities—if, that is to say, we were to leave ourselves with something which had no qualities or relations at all—we should not be in a position to make any statement about it. Nor can we conceive of something which has no qualities at all. The substance of the desk turns out, then, to be no more rewarding to a mind which is in search of something stable, fixed and definite to come to rest on, something which can serve as the object of certain knowledge, than the supposed qualities of the substance. A similar treatment, Plato holds, can be extended to all the familiar objects of the common sense world. The analysis is familiar in philosophy and has usually been undertaken in the interests of some form of philosophical Idealism. It has usually, that is to say, been designed to support the conclusion which maintains that everything that exists is mental in the sense either of being in a mind, or of being dependent on a mind, or of existing only in relation to a mind. I shall say something of this view, which has been perhaps the dominant view in philosophy, in a later chapter.[1]

Of What is there Knowledge?

Plato is concerned to draw a different conclusion. The familiar objects of the everyday world cannot, he holds, be wholly real. If they were, we should be able to obtain certain knowledge about them, affirming, for example, that a substance was so and so, or that it had such and such qualities in some sense in which it did not have the opposite qualities. But, as we have seen, we are not entitled to say that we possess knowledge of this kind. Here the point ought to be made— though I hope to return to it later[2]—that it is no answer to this contention to say that we have scientific knowledge of familiar things and that scientific knowledge is certain and true. For the question arises what are the objects of which scientific knowledge gives us information? Consider, for example, the kind of knowledge that physics and chemistry give us. To *what* does that knowledge relate; of *what* is it? Most physicists would answer that it is knowledge of the relation between things or events or phenomena. It tells us, for example, that the relation between hydrogen and oxygen is such that two parts of the former and one of the latter produce or *are* water; it does not tell us what water is, or what oxygen is, or what hydrogen is. Or it tells us that the attraction between bodies in empty space varies inversely with the square of the distance between them; but it does not tell us what the attracted bodies are. It tells us that a solid object is analyzable

[1] See Chapter 4, pp. 87–89.

[2] See Chapter 4, pp. 78–83.

into atoms and that atoms are charges of electricity; but it does not tell us what charges of electricity are.

Procedure of the Sciences

Let us develop this last point. The typical procedure of the sciences of physics and chemistry is to take an apparently solid object and to represent it as being composed of molecules which are, in their turn, analyzable into their elements. The elements are composed of atoms which are (or were until recently) supposed to consist of protons and electrons. Now we are, it is obvious, entitled to ask in regard to the molecules, the elements, the atoms, the protons and the electrons, or in regard to whatever other kind of entity may now or at some future time become fashionable as the ultimate constituent of matter, precisely the same questions as those which we put above in regard to the desk. For these, too, are presumably substances of some kind which possess qualities, even if in the case of the electron the qualities are austerely mathematical, being limited to position in space and velocity of movement. We must ask, then, whether these qualities, considered in and by themselves, are intelligible, and whether the substance which is supposed to possess them can be known independently of the qualities, just as we did when we were considering the brownness, the hardness and the substance of the desk. And these questions could, so far as one can see, be appropriately asked whatever the nature of the constituents into which matter may ultimately be analyzed. Reverting, then, to Plato's analysis, we shall find him pointing out that you cannot have certain knowledge of qualities which are fluctuating and relative, precisely because the thing which possesses those qualities cannot truly be said to *be* anything at all, since it is always half-way on the road to becoming something else. Hence, Plato insisted that the familiar world must be regarded as a world of *becoming*, rather than a world of *being*, since it never truly *is* anything at all. We cannot, then, he concluded, have certain knowledge of the familiar world which is revealed to us in sense experience, precisely because that world is not wholly real.

Nevertheless, he proceeded to argue, we *do* possess certain and definite knowledge. The spheres in which we most obviously possess it are those of mathematics and logic. I do, that is to say, quite certainly know that $a^2 - b^2 = (a + b)$

$(a - b)$, that the whole is greater than its part, that a thing cannot both be and not be, that if P implies Q and Q implies R, then P implies R, and so on.

We also possess it, Plato held, in the sphere of ethics; thus we do, he maintained, certainly know that right is better than wrong and that we ought to try to live a good life. We even know, in a general sort of way, what makes a good life, since we know justice to be better than injustice, kindness than cruelty, honesty than deceit. But, as we have already seen, we can only truly and certainly know something if that something really exists, exists, that is to say, unchangeably and in its own right and remains itself and which, by virtue of the fact that it does so exist and remain itself, permits itself to be known. The conclusion is that the spheres of logic and of ethics are in some way the homes of—one would like to say that they contain but for the misleading spatial metaphor involved—real things. What, then, are real things? If the familiar world does not provide us with a standard of reality, where are we to look for it?

Plato's Conception of Reality

For an answer to the question, what things are real, Plato turns first to a consideration of those qualities which things possess in common. Sheets, snow, cream, are all white, but what, he asks, is whiteness? The same as any one of them? Obviously not. The same as all of them? Again obviously not, since the experience of thinking about whiteness is quite different from that of thinking about all the white things that there are, or even about all the white things that we know. If whiteness is neither any one white thing, nor all the white things that there are, is it perhaps an idea or conception in my mind? This, I imagine, is the answer which most people would be inclined to give, but it is not Plato's. Let us consider some of the objections to it.

(1) If whiteness is an idea in my mind, then when I think about whiteness, the whiteness of cream, for example, the whiteness I am thinking about is something in or belonging to me. But the cream is presumably independent of me. How, then, can the whiteness belong to the cream? Again, if the whiteness of the cream is a concept in my mind, what are we to say of its liquidity, its smoothness and its taste qualities? It seems most unlikely that they should really belong to the

cream, while its whiteness belongs to in the sense of being an idea in my mind. But if we say that they, too, belong to in the sense of being ideas in my mind, it is difficult to see what is left out there in the external world, since *all* the qualities of the cream will by the same reasoning be concepts or ideas in my mind. What, then, is cream apart from its qualities? Presumably a substance; but a substance without qualities is something which, even if it exists, cannot be referred to. The view that the qualities of the cream are in fact concepts in my mind will be considered in the next chapter.[1] But unless we are prepared to go all the way with those who hold this view and affirm that *all* the qualities which we believe ourselves to perceive are in our minds, with the corollary that we never succeed in thinking about a world outside ourselves at all, we shall not be justified in giving this answer in regard to whiteness.

(2) When we think, we normally take it for granted that there is something other than our minds and their thoughts *about* which we are thinking—something, that is to say, which constitutes what is known as the *object* of our thoughts. Now, if we agree that this is the case in regard to the squareness of the table, the date of the Battle of Waterloo and the chemical formula for water, to take examples from the spheres of geometry, history and science respectively, why should we arbitrarily reject this view in its bearing upon the whiteness of cream? If, in other words, we hold that when we think there is an object to be thought about which is other than our thinking, why should it not be so in the case of whiteness?

(3) If it were true that whiteness were a concept in the mind, then if all minds were abolished, cream would cease to be white. Let us consider a hypothetical case in which the last human being possessing consciousness is engaged in thinking (I am sorry that the example is so unplausible) about the whiteness of cream. He is, we will suppose, the victim of a disease whose effect is to induce a gradual fade-out of consciousness. As he contemplates the white cream, the vividness of his sensation grows fainter and fainter, until, finally, he ceases to be able to see it at all. Are we, then, to suppose that during this process the cream *itself* grows gradually less and less white, until eventually, as the last human consciousness fades out of the universe, it ceases altogether to be white?

[1] See Chapter 4, pp. 76–78.

This seems, to say the least of it, unlikely. There are, of course, certain philosophical theories which do maintain precisely this,[1] but the onus of proof rests upon them, and they have certainly not been proven.

(4) If when I think about the whiteness of cream, I am thinking about a concept in my mind, and if when you think about the whiteness of cream, you are thinking about a concept in your mind, we never, it is obvious, succeed in thinking about the same thing. If this is the case, it is difficult to understand how we ever intelligibly communicate with one another.

Plato concludes that whiteness is what he calls a Form—something, that is to say, which is not *in* the mind, but is recognized and thought about by the mind. This Form, whiteness, manifests itself in all white things, and, by virtue of its manifestation, bestows upon them that quality by reason of which we call them white. For why is it, Plato asks, that we describe by the same epithet things which are as different as cream, snow and sheets? He answers that it is because the mind recognizes in each of these things the presence of a common element which is due to the fact that they "participate" in, or "partake" of the same quality, whiteness.

The Forms as Ideals and Standards

But the Form is more than the source of the common qualities of the things that manifest it. It is also the perfect example or type to which they all more or less imperfectly approximate and the standard by reference to which their degree of approximation is judged, while its perfection constitutes the end, or goal, to which, metaphorically, they may be said to aspire. There is nothing that we feel which is so hot that we could not imagine something which is a little hotter; there is no sky in June so blue that it does not point onward to a bluer; no music so lovely that it does not suggest the thought of a greater loveliness; no drawn line so straight that we could not theoretically conceive it to be straighter—in fact, we must concede that no visible straight line ever is straight, for if, as Euclid does, we define a straight line as that which has length without breadth, then we must remind ourselves that every straight line that has ever been drawn has some breadth and is not, therefore, ideally straight. The application of any geometrical truth to the figures that actually exist in the sensible

[1] See Chapter 4, pp. 87–89.

world is subject to the same element of error. Thus, geo-
metricians demonstrate a number of truths about triangles—
as for example, that their three interior angles are equal to
two right angles or that, if two of their sides are equal, the
angles at the base will also be equal. Now, all these statements
depend for their being completely true upon the figure to
which they purport to apply being really a triangle. But in
fact we know that no triangle that has ever been drawn really
is a triangle, since it is composed of lines that have breadth
as well as length and are not quite straight, and which meet in
points which have magnitude as well as position and are not,
therefore, really points. All the triangles that we have ever
seen are trying, as Plato would say, to be as much like triangles as the visible and tangible subject-matter of which
they are constructed—whether it be chalk or pencil or ink or
string or wood—permits. In other words, they approximate to
the perfect triangle but are not themselves perfectly triangular.
It follows that none of the truths which geometry demon-
strates about triangles is quite true in its relation to the triangles we see. Nevertheless, the truths are quite true. Of what,
then, Plato asks, are they true? His answer is that they are
true of the Form of the triangle—that is to say, of the perfect
triangle which is the standard by reference to which the degree
of triangularity of all visible triangles is judged, and which
he thinks of metaphorically as constituting the goal or end
which all existing triangles seek to realize, trying to be as like
or to embody as much of the triangularity of the perfect triangle as the stuff of which they are made permits.

In its application to triangles this notion of the Form as a
goal or end is a metaphor; but there are other spheres in which
a mode of speaking which is here metaphorical becomes literal
—in which, that is to say, we can think of the imperfect
approximations of the familiar world as really endeavoring to
become less imperfect by realizing ever more completely the
Form which is incompletely manifested in them.

The Sphere of Aesthetics

In these spheres the Forms perform not only the function
of sources of the common qualities, but serve also in a quite
literal sense as goals or ideals, and it is in fact with reference
to these spheres that the development of Plato's theory mainly
takes place. The first of these spheres is that of aesthetics,

which deals with the philosophy of art. What, it asks, is the
common element in virtue of which we appreciate and delight
in good pictures, good music, good poetry and also good
tapestry, good china, good furniture and the various *objets
d'art* which art dealers sell and collectors buy? The collectors
buy them because they have value, but in what does their
value consist? Their rarity? But many things which are rare
are not valuable. Their age? Stones are old, yet nobody values
them. Plato answers that the source of the value of these objects, the element which is common to good pictures, good
music and good poetry, as well as to good tapestry, good china
and good furniture, is beauty, and that the source of the
power which certain objects have to move us aesthetically
and to give us delight is their beauty. He adds that the source
of this beauty which is manifested as a common quality in
music, poetry and works of art and also in old furniture, old
china, old tapestry—one has, alas, to insist on the word "old";
beauty does not easily grace men's handiwork in these spheres
in the twentieth century—is the Form of beauty. The validity
of the answer is not affected by the fact that one man will
consider to be beautiful what others do not, and that the
fashion of one age will reject the most admired works of its
predecessor; for it is a presupposition of the answer that some
things really *are* beautiful, whether we see the beauty in
them or not, and that when two people differ in regard to
the degree of beauty possessed by a work of art, one of them
will be right and the other wrong; or, more precisely, the
judgment of one will possess a greater degree of accuracy
than that of the other. It follows that many people are blind
to the beauty which objects possess—for example, the people
who find Bach's Fugues dull—while others will falsely believe
beauty to be present in objects from which it is, in fact,
absent; for example, in the pictures of bathing beauties on the
covers of the summer issues of magazines. The ability to
discern beauty when it is present is good taste, and good
taste, like any other capacity, can be trained and cultivated.
In fact it needs to be, our natural and instinctive tastes being
almost invariably bad—one of the results, conceivably, of the
Fall. (It is an odd thing, by the way, that while we are all
accustomed to the view that human beings are sinful—that is
to say, are naturally tempted to do and prefer the bad to the
good—we are shocked into incredulity by the announcement
that they are aesthetically blind and naturally prefer the ugly

to the beautiful. Yet, granted the Fall, it is reasonable to suppose that, as the theologians would put it, we bear upon us the marks of original aesthetic as well as of original moral sin.) It is, then, a corollary of Plato's view that good taste does not come by chance, or nature, but can be acquired only as the result of a long and laborious process of training and experience. But what is meant by saying of an object that it is beautiful? The answer we have so far given is that it partakes of the Form of beauty, or that the Form of beauty is manifested in it, and that the manifestations of the Form are the source of the common quality which all beautiful objects possess. The Form is also the ideal after which they strive. What meaning, it may be asked, can be given to this conception of an object as "striving", even if the object be a work of art which is "striving" to be beautiful?

The Function of the Artist

The answer involves a reference to the artist. How does the artist differ from the ordinary man? By reason of his capacities, first, to discern beauty and, secondly, to embody it in his work of art, whether it be in sound or paint or stone or steel or film or, if he be a poet, in words. We speak of the first capacity under the name of inspiration or vision; to the second we refer as execution, skill or technique. The artist, then, is one who in the first place perceives the significance of combinations of shape and color which escapes the ordinary man. The great writer and, more particularly, the great poet strips the film of familiarity from our eyes and gives us, if only for a moment, a fresh vision of the strangeness and wonder of the world and of the brief life of man. But the vision is not enough; it must receive concrete shape and form, for without these, though there may be artists, there are no works of art. To some the work of embodiment comes easily, as Mozart is said to have conceived in advance the plan of the movement of a Symphony and then to have proceeded to write it down, transcribing what was already in his mind; to others it is beset with difficulty; thus Beethoven wrought and wrestled with his material, trying out first this combination and then that, as he strove painfully to forge the musical phrase that would embody his idea with the minimum of distortion. But whether he produces easily or with difficulty, the great artist can never feel wholly satisfied with the result of his efforts, for he works with an intractable material which, being of the stuff of this world, whether it be sound or stone or paint or steel, can never be a wholly adequate vehicle for the ideas and combinations that derive from another; can never, as Plato would say, wholly manifest the Form of beauty. The artist, then, does the best he can with the material at his disposal and in the work of art seeks to show forth as much of beauty as, given the hampering effect of the material and the limitations of his own vision, he is able to reveal.

Thus, beauty is a goal as well as a source; it is a goal for the artist because it is his vision of it which is the inspiration that drives the artist to create; it is a goal for the work of art in which the artist seeks to embody as much of his vision as the limitations of his skill and of the material permit; it is a goal for the spectator whose vision is pointed forward by the beauty of the picture to the possibility of a greater beauty beyond, of which the picture gives him his first faltering realization.

Value, then, the value of beauty, is not only a static Form which confers their common aesthetic quality upon the objects we call beautiful; it is dynamic and active in the world, driving men forward to realize it as creators, and to comprehend it as recipients of the beauty of works of art. It follows that art in all its forms is the attempt to bring to birth, however imperfectly, in the changing shapes and sounds of this world, the Forms of a world of value which is permanent and perfect.

The world of value which art seeks to embody is, according to Plato, the real world; the familiar world of things and people in which the Forms are embodied is a world of shadows or copies, deriving such reality as it possesses from its reflection of the real world, which is as substance to shadow and original to imitation.

In illustrating this conception I have referred chiefly to the arts of music and painting not only because I am more familiar with these arts, but because the application of the theory is more readily seen in relation to them. But that the view of the world of art as the reality which is at once the ideal to which representations in this world endeavor with more or less success to approximate and the standard by reference to which their degree of approximation can be estimated, can be applied to other arts which, in subject-matter, technique and appeal, are more closely interfused with the things of this world, the following quotation from the conclusion of Somerset Maugham's book *Theatre* bears witness. A great actress, fresh from a new success, is reflecting upon her performance in relation to the effect it has produced upon her audience.

" 'We,' she says—the actors and the actresses—'are the meaning of their'—the audience's—'lives. We take their silly little emotions and turn them into art, out of them we create beauty, and their significance is that they form the audience we must have to fulfil ourselves. They are the instruments on which we play, and what is an instrument without somebody to play on it?'

"The notion exhilarated her, and for a moment or two she savoured of it with satisfaction. Her brain seemed miraculously lucid.

" 'Roger says we don't exist. Why, it's only we who do exist. They are the shadows and we give them substance. We are the symbols of all this confused, aimless struggling that they call life, and it's only the symbol which is real. They say acting is only make-believe. That make-believe is the only reality.'

"Thus Julia out of her own head framed anew the Platonic theory of ideas."

In the case of pictures it is the canvas, in that of music the sound, in that of acting the audience, which performs the office of instrument or raw material, which the artist uses for the showing forth of the Form.

One of the most famous passages in philosophy, or indeed in the literature of any language, is that which occurs at the beginning of the Seventh Book of Plato's *Republic*, in which he likens the position of men and women on earth to that of prisoners in a cave, so placed that they cannot see real things, but only the images of them reflected on the wall of the cave by the light of a fire. Never having seen anything which is not an image, they take the images to be reality, and do not suspect that it is an immaterial reality which gives to the images such status, the status of reflections, as they possess. I have not here space to describe the simile of the Cave, as it is called, nor would a bald summary do justice to the compelling power of the passage. I can only recommend those who would study philosophy for themselves to read and reflect upon it as an attempt by a great philosopher, who is also a great artist, to illuminate under the guise of metaphor the conception of reality of which the theory of art I have so briefly sketched is one outstanding application.

The Sphere of Morals

The other sphere in which the Form stands forth as not only the ground of the common qualities of things but as an end or ideal to be striven for is the sphere of ethics. In this sphere, moreover, the Form is further revealed as the source of that in us which strives after the ideal. Ethics is the theory of right and wrong; it seeks, among other things, to discover the basis and compulsive power of what we call duty. One of the questions with which it concerns itself is why men alone among created beings recognize the distinction between "I want" and "I ought". Ethics is, as I have explained, one of the main branches of philosophy, and I hope to devote a chapter[1] to a discussion of some of its problems. Among these is the question whether the principles of right and wrong, good and bad, are merely human conceptions, descriptions of the ways in which our minds work, or rationalizations of expediency and laziness—we call things right on this view because they conduce to our advantage or to the advantage of our community—or are independent principles or factors in the fundamental make-up of the universe which we recognize and try, however imperfectly, to realize in our lives. The first answer exemplifies what is called a subjective, the second an objective view of ethics. This problem will be discussed in Chapter 5.

It follows from what has been said that Plato's view is an objective one. Goodness is, for him, a Form—the *Republic* is ostensibly devoted to an examination of the manifestation of the Form of justice in the lives of individuals and communities—which is independent of the institutions, codes, acts and characters of men that we recognize to be good, and which confers upon them such goodness as they exhibit. In this *rôle* the Form is the common source which manifests itself in all the qualities which we recognize as good, and by reason of our recognition characterize all the things and people to which the qualities belong as moral, just or praiseworthy. But, as in the case of the Form of beauty, it is more than the source of common qualities. First, it is an ideal, an ideal not determined or created by the human mind, but recognized

[1] See Chapter 5.

by it. We realize that no single institution is wholly or perfectly just, no human character wholly and perfectly good. But how could we know that they are not—how, in other words, could we recognize the fact of their partial imperfection, if we had not in our minds a conception of the ideal perfection to which they approximate and in their falling short of which the fact of their imperfection consists, just as we should not know darkness to be dark, unless we also knew what light was? Secondly, the Form is a standard by reference to which we judge and assess the degree of the "falling short". Thirdly, it is the inspiring principle which impels us to seek to realize it as an ideal in our actions and our lives. It may seem far-fetched to talk of the triangle that we draw as seeking to realize ever more of the principle of triangularity which it manifests, but it is perfectly natural to think of the good man as trying to achieve a more perfect degree of goodness. Not only does he recognize the Form of goodness as a goal or ideal and seek to pursue it, but it is also the Form which, as mani-fested in his soul, inspires the efforts which he makes to live a better life and so to approximate ever more closely to the ideal. In Plato's theory the Form of goodness occupies a peculiar position among the Forms, in that the medium of its manifestations is not wood as with the form of squareness, or linen as with the form of whiteness, or paint and canvas as with the form of beauty, but is the lives and characters of men and women.

Transcendence and Immanence

This peculiarity illustrates and so helps us to comprehend the two aspects under which Plato conceives of the Forms, the aspect Transcendence and that of Immanence. Trans-cendence and Immanence are words which are constantly turning up in theological writings—God, we are told, is both transcendent and immanent; He is outside the world, yet He is also present in the hearts of men—and stand for notions which are not easy either to understand or to convey. Both notions are comprised in Plato's conception of the Forms and are strikingly illustrated by the Form of goodness in its relation to and its manifestation in human beings. First, the Forms are a world apart in themselves; they constitute, in fact, an independent reality, and nothing that happens to the familiar world of things can possibly affect them. Plato says somewhere that if the whole world of sensible things were swept away, the Forms would remain unaffected. In a famous passage in the *Republic* he represents the Forms as a hierarchy leading up to the Form of the Good, which is the single, unifying principle of the universe. The Form of the Good in the real world is likened to the sun in the visible world, in that, just as the sun is both the cause of the existence of the things we see, for through it they grow, and of our seeing them, for through it there is light, so the Form of the Good is both the fundamental principle of reality and as such transcendent, and also the cause of our knowledge of reality and as such immanent. How does it come to be the second of these things? By reason of its presence in our own souls. The good man is not only good but recognizes and aspires after goodness when he perceives it, and while this recognition is achieved only in virtue of such goodness as he possesses, it also acts as his incentive to achieve a higher degree of goodness, to become, in fact, better. Here, then, we contemplate the Form under its second aspect, that of immanence, as present, that is to say, in what Plato calls the world of becoming, the particular medium for its manifestation being the soul of man. Reality, then, is not wholly aloof and apart; it is also the innermost essence of ourselves. Generalizing this, we may say that in Plato's universe the Forms are not merely the constitutive principle of reality, although they do, indeed, constitute reality; they are also, by virtue of their manifestation in the things of the familiar world, the cause of the qualities which the familiar world is seen to possess.

Difficulties in Plato's Conception

We may well ask how this can be. Indeed, the commonest criticism of Plato's Theory of Forms turns on precisely this double aspect of Transcendence and Immanence. I have not the space for an adequate treatment of these difficult questions, but it is worth while to pause to see what the criticism is.

Let us suppose, first, that the Forms are transcendent or, to put the same point in more familiar language, that the real world is utterly remote and aloof from the familiar world. Then the universe falls into two halves between which there is no connection. There is, in fact, not one universe; there are two. Now there must, one would say, be *some* sense in which there is a single universe; there must, that is to say, be a whole of all that there is, which somehow includes and holds together whatever there is. If, then, the familiar world and Plato's real world fall apart, so that we have not one but two worlds on our hands, then the mind is led forward by the necessities of its own demand for unity to postulate a third world which is more inclusive than either, of which both Plato's world and the familiar world are aspects. This third world would be the real universe and Plato's so-called real world would only be a part or aspect of the universe; it would not, therefore, be itself reality. If, moreover, we do take this view, what are we to make of Plato's often-repeated statements that it is the presence of the Forms in the familiar thing which confers upon it the qualities in virtue of which it owns such reality as belongs to it? How *could* the Forms be present in the familiar world if they are wholly apart from it?

Now let us suppose, secondly, that the Forms are immanent in the familiar world. We are then faced with the apparently insoluble problem, how can that which is wholly real be the cause of the being of, nay more, constitute the innermost core and essence of, that which is semi-real? If whiteness is wholly real and snow is only semi-real, whence does the element of unreality or semi-reality intrude itself? How, in any event, one may ask, can reality become or cause to be what is less real than itself? It is not possible to pursue these difficult questions here. They raise a similar problem to one which will be familiar to some readers in another form, the problem, namely, of the theological explanation of the world. God, we are told, created the world and from time to time actively intervenes in its affairs by a succession of mighty acts of which, according to Christian doctrine, the sending of His Son into the world in the form of a human being was the most outstanding. God, then, is the sole cause of the existence of the world and He is still in some sense present and active in it. Yet the world is imperfect; it is, indeed, shot through with evil and suffering. Moreover, being filled with change and decay it cannot, as Plato insists, be wholly real. How, then, one must ask, if God is perfect can He be the immanent cause of a world that is imperfect? How can God who is changeless be the motive principle of a world which is changing and decaying?

I have just excused myself from pursuing these questions on the ground of lack of space. The excuse, I am afraid, was hypocritical in the sense that no treatment, however profound or prolonged, has yet succeeded in resolving these difficulties. It may be doubted whether any treatment ever will.

I have dwelt upon the cases of the artist and of the good man because, although we may totally fail to understand how the solution has been effected, they do nevertheless exhibit the solution in practice. For the artist, beauty is transcendent; it is that which he seeks to realize and to bring to birth in the familiar world and this beauty is something other than himself. Yet, the perceptiveness of beauty is also in him and provides him with the insight and inspiration without which the creation of works of art would be impossible; beauty is also embodied in the successful work of art which he creates. In both these latter senses beauty is immanent in the world.

Similarly, for the good man goodness is an end in itself and duty a law which he recognizes as being independent of himself; they are as essential elements in the fundamental order of the universe as are the laws of mathematics and physics. In this sense goodness is transcendent. At the same time goodness is present in him in the sense that it is only because he is already a moral being that he feels the pull of duty; only in so far as he is already a good man that he wants to be a better one. It is also embodied in the good acts that he performs, as is justice in the institutions which he establishes.

Political Corollaries

My account of Plato's theory of Ideas or Forms was partly undertaken in order to introduce his theory of politics. An understanding of the metaphysics was, I suggested, a necessary preliminary to a sympathetic approach to the provisions of his ideal State. These deserve a chapter to themselves even for the purposes of summary. I do not, however, propose to summarize them here, if only because I do not want to give my readers any excuse for refusing to follow my advice and read the *Republic* for themselves. I propose, then, to say no more than is necessary to bring Plato's political theory within the framework of the metaphysical picture which has already been sketched, while seeking at the same time to exonerate him from the charges of Totalitarianism, and even of Fascism, that have in recent years been brought against him.

Plato's Account of the Soul

It is necessary to preface Plato's political theory with a brief account of his psychology. Plato makes a three-fold division of the soul of man into a reasoning part, a spirited part and a desiring part. The reasoning, which he calls the first part of the soul, includes what we should class under the name of reason or intellect and also a more vaguely conceived quality which we denote by the word "insight". Insight is the faculty of penetrating below the surface of things to the reality that underlies them. The word, as commonly used, stands also for the good aesthetic taste of the man who discerns and appreciates what is beautiful in art and the good moral taste of the man who recognizes what is valuable in conduct and character. The reasoning part of the soul knows the Forms; knows, therefore, reality. The reasoning part of the soul, as Plato conceives it, contains also a dynamic element. The "reasonable man" who is Plato's philosopher, does not merely recognize the good and distinguish it from the bad; he is also impelled to strive after the good and to eschew the bad that he recognizes. The second part of the soul, the spirited, is chiefly exemplified in the military man and is expressed in the qualities of courage, ferocity, fortitude, loyalty and patriotism which are traditionally associated with him, both for good and for evil. The goods which the "spirited" man craves are honor and glory; but he has not the discernment to discover which are the ends which justify the display of his loyalty and his courage, or which excuse his ferocity; in a word, he desires honor yet does not know what is honorable. Left to himself, he would just as cheerfully fight in an unjust as in a just cause. The soldier, then, must be under the instruction and guidance of the "philosopher" who, by virtue of his knowledge of what is good, knows what ends justify the display of the soldierly virtues. In Plato's State the military man acts as a kind of bodyguard to the philosopher, supplying him with the power to subdue and to rule those in whom the third part of the soul in predominant. If we liken the philosopher to the engine driver who knows where to drive the engine of society, the spirited man is the steam that makes it go.

The Third Part of the Soul

Thirdly, there is the part of the soul that craves and desires. This is conceived as a kind of passional ragbag in which all the desires and impulses originate, rise into consciousness and clamor for satisfaction, the desires for respectability and display as well as those for food and sex; ambition, envy and avarice as well as boasting, snobbery and malice. Unless checked and disciplined, these desires dominate our nature; or rather, first one and then another dominates, as each happens at a particular moment to get the mastery over the others. A man ruled by the third part of his soul is, then, like a boat which having lost its rudder drifts first this way and then that according to the strongest puff of wind that fills its sails, or the strongest current that deflects its keel. Such a boat is incapable of pursuing any planned or definite course and, voyaging at haphazard, is unable to avoid the reefs which lie across its course. Inevitably, then, it comes sooner or later upon destruction. In just the same way the man whose life is dominated by impulse and desire is driven first this way and then that; today he is all for wine and women, tomorrow for plain living and high thinking; in the morning a serious student sitting at his books; in the evening a gay dog getting tight at a night club; one day agog with the spirit of adventure and planning to go to the Pole or to climb Mount Everest, the next opting for a quiet life and looking for a wife with whom he may settle down, found a family and achieve respectability. Such a man, swept by one impulse after another, attracted first by this end and then by that, is incapable of the prolonged and purposive effort necessary to realize any one of them. Like Dryden's *Zimri*, he is

" . . . everything by starts, and nothing long:
But in the course of one revolving moon
Was chemist, fiddler, statesman and buffoon;
Then all for women, dining, rhyming, drinking,
Besides ten thousand freaks that died in thinking."

Hence arises the need for reason to control and command desire, not denying the desires their legitimate satisfaction, but disciplining them so that no one obtains a larger share of satisfaction than is due to it having regard to the equally legitimate claims of the rest, and dovetailing them one into another, so that their energy is harnessed to the service of one dominating purpose, such as the desire to serve the community or to become a better man. Thus the man in whom reason rules is like a boat guided by a helmsman who employs rudder and compass to steer to a definite objective. He uses the power of the winds when they suit his purpose but confronts them when they do not; goes with the current when it is favorable, struggles with it and overcomes it when it sets against his course. We should, then—and here is Plato's formula for the practical living of the good life—allow the first part of the soul to guide and dominate the third, enlisting the fire and spirit of the second to assist it in its task of control and dominance. In the *Republic* the virtue of Justice is identified with the contented performance of its proper function by each of the three parts of the soul. The just soul is one in which the reasoning part guides, the spirited part assists it to enforce its guidance, and the desiring or appetitive part accepts the discipline of the reasoning part. Justice in the soul consists of the achievement, the maintenance and the functioning in daily life of this right relationship of parts.

According to the part of his soul which is dominant, so will be the general character and disposition of the man. He in whom the first part of the soul predominates is the philosopher, as Plato calls him, who is also the Guardian of the State[1]; he in whom the second, the soldier or warrior, while the ordinary citizen is portrayed as the man in whom the third part of the soul dominates. For the ordinary citizen is predominantly a man of impulse and desire; he does the work of the community and produces the commodities which are necessary for its existence, but does these things to the end that his desires may be satisfied and his belly filled. He is the good *bourgeois* all the world over, *l'homme moyen sensuel*. Governed by the stomach and pocket view of life, he seeks money that he may be safe and safety that he may be comfortable. And what is to be comfortable? To satisfy those of one's desires which may be indulged without forfeiting the good opinion of the neighbors, to have as good a time as is possible while "keeping up with the Jones's". Hence Plato assigns the *bourgeois* respectability-loving citizen to the

[1] See below, pp. 61–64.

class of those in whom the third part of the soul is predominant. He desires neither the wisdom of the philosopher, which is the good of the first, nor the hard honor-loving life of the soldier, which is the good of the second part of the soul. He is neither sage, Communist nor Fascist. He desires only to be left in comfort to pursue his women, fill his belly, found his family, sleep after his round of golf on Sunday and go about his business during the week. It is interesting to observe that Plato assigns to the third class both those whom we should call employers and those whom we call workers, since both are engaged in working and producing in order to achieve money and security. A gentleman is, for Plato, as he was for the Victorians, one who is engaged in some non-productive activity.

Classes of State

Plato's political theory is closely modelled on his psychology. The soul of man being, for him, a microcosm of the State, what is true of the soul is, given a few obviously necessary modifications, true of the State. Just as there are three kinds of soul, so there are three kinds of State and just as the nature of the soul as a whole is determined by the part which is dominant in it, so that there are predominantly reasoning, predominantly spirited and predominantly appetitive souls, so the nature of the State is determined by the class of man who is dominant in it, so that we get philosophic, military or business man's States, each of which reflects in its general character or constitution, the nature of the class of man which is predominant and holds rule in it. Thus the State which is dominated by men in whose souls the second part is predominant will be an aggressive State in which military glory and power are the goods of the ruling class. It is impossible, as one reads Plato's vivid account of these States (they are called "timocratic", or honor-loving States) in the Eighth book of the *Republic* not to be reminded of contemporary Fascist countries. Yet Nazi Germany, though it recalls, is clearly a perversion of, Plato's honor-loving State, a perversion of what Plato regarded as itself a perversion.

The State which is dominated by men of the third class is identified by Plato with democracy, and his treatment involves a vigorous attack upon democracy by which many good liberals and democrats have been affronted. Just as those who are governed by the third part of the soul are money-lovers, since money is wanted for the satisfaction of their desires, so States in which such men predominate will value money and give power to those who are skilled at making money. As one reads, one is irresistibly reminded of the American worship of the dollar, of the dominance of wealth in American politics, of the all-pervasive standard of valuation in terms of money—how much does it cost? how much is he worth?—which impels the American to tell you the price of everything, while realizing, the cynic might add, the true value of nothing, and the Nazi's gibes at the pluto-democracies. In the soul of the democratic man the desires hold sway and as they arise, first one and then the other without rhyme or reason, they clamor for gratification without reference to the good of the whole or to any coherent plan which reason may have designed for the living of the good life. In just the same way the democratic State is dominated by whatever party or interest happens to get the upper hand at the elections and is run with the sole purpose of furthering the interests of the victorious party with perhaps an occasional sop (one is reminded of the dole) or an anodyne (jazz or football pools) to keep the oppressed or dissatisfied elements quiet. In the democratic man's soul any part deems itself capable of assuming the governance of the whole; so, too, in the democratic State every class, however uneducated, considers itself fit to assume the duties of government. Thus, the democratic State is the arch offender against Plato's principle of Justice, in that, instead of everybody going about his own business, the business which he is fitted by training and disposition to perform and which is assigned to him precisely because it is for this that he *has* been trained and *is* fitted, everybody in a democracy meddles with everybody else's concerns, the business man aspiring to govern and the workers being conscripted to fight. I resist the temptation to enlarge on the features of this formidable indictment, partly because I would not spoil the artistry of Plato's picture by an inadequate summary, partly because, as a good democrat myself, I am chary of presenting too forcibly the devil's advocacy. For there is, of course, a defense and in a later chapter[1] some part of it will be attempted. Plato's indictment of democracy is partly designed to throw into high relief the virtues of the remaining class of State, that which is dom-

[1] See Chapter 6, pp. 152–159.

inated by men in whom the first part of the soul is predominant, that is to say, by those who are guided by reason. These are Plato's philosophers and this is his ideal State. I have already excused myself from giving an account of its provisions. It remains, however, to link the theory of the ideal State with the theory of Forms already described, in order to show how the politics fits into the framework of the metaphysics.

Plato's Guardians

The Guardians are those in whom the first part of the soul, the reasoning part, controls the rest. So far as the practice of living is concerned, it is the function of reason to control the passions, harnessing them to the performance of whatever task, disciplining them to the leading of whatever way of life reason prescribes. The passions being tamed and controlled, reason is free to perform her proper task, undistracted by their solicitations. What is reason's proper task and what the way of living which reason prescribes?

Plato's answer is that the proper task of reason is the exploration and contemplation of reality, and that so far as the practice of living is concerned, reason is content to prescribe the leading of such a life as may be necessary to this end. Now reality, as we have seen, consists of Forms. Therefore, those in whom the reasoning part of the soul is in control, Plato's philosopher-Guardians, will seek to know and to contemplate the Forms. There are many passages in Plato in praise of the contemplative life which belong to the literature of mysticism; this is one of the most persistent strains in Plato's thought, which I must be excused from following here. Plato also describes in some detail the education which much be given to the Guardians with the object of wheeling the soul as he puts it, "round from the perishing world" to the "contemplation of the real world and the brightest part thereof".

Our concern here is with the political implications of this recipe for living. It is to the State that the philosophers owe the training and the education in virtue of which they are enabled to attain to a knowledge of the Forms. In addition to educating, the State maintains them. (There are some interesting provisions for a communist order of society describing how the Guardians will live together, holding all things in common.)

The philosophers, then, owe an obligation to the State, an obligation which lays upon them a duty. Their desire is to devote their lives to the contemplation of reality upon which their hearts are stayed, but accepting the obligation and recognizing the duty, they relinquish from time to time their contemplation of the real world and for prescribed periods devote themselves to the governance of the State, coming back, as Plato puts it, to the Cave to consort with its prisoners and to occupy themselves with its affairs. Contemplating reality they are philosophers; guiding and governing the State they are Guardians. The vision of reality revealed to them as philosophers has shown them the Forms of justice and goodness not as imperfectly manifested in the institutions and characters of men, but as these Forms are in themselves, as, that is to say, fundamental features of reality. The memory of this vision abides with them when they return to the Cave and, in the light of it, they draw up rules for the guidance of the community. These rules constitute the laws of the ideal State and, since they embody the Forms of goodness and justice, they are the best possible laws, being framed in the light of the knowledge of the best.

That Philosophers must be Kings

Several features which have been touched upon in the previous discussion are embodied in this conception. First, there is the double relation of Transcendence and Immanence which obtains between the Forms and the familiar world; the Forms are transcendent, but they are also immanent in the sense that they are manifested in the laws of the ideal State by reason of the knowledge of them possessed by the Guardians, their framers. They inform its legislation and make it what it is. The relation of the world of reality to the world of politics is not, therefore, merely a relation of transcendent aloofness, since reality enters into and informs the arrangements of the good State, as it does the life of the good man.

Secondly, the good which is embodied in the legislative provisions and institutions of the good State is a dynamic good in the sense that, while no State that has ever existed upon earth is perfect, every imperfect State seeks, and seeks by reason of the goodness that it already embodies, to correct its imperfections and to increase its goodness. It seeks, then, to approximate ever more closely to the perfect State as

its goal or ideal. I say that the State seeks, but, more precisely, it is the men who rule the State who seek, since in the
degree to which they approach to the ideal condition of
Plato's Guardians, to that degree do they strive to make the
State a more worthy manifestation of the ideal which they, as
imperfect rulers, imperfectly glimpse. Thus, a good community like a good man seeks continuously to become a better
one.

Now this result, in Plato's view, can be achieved only
in so far as men of thought and men of action—instead
of being, as they have been in every civilization, different
species or sorts or men living different sorts of lives—are
the same men; for it is only in so far as the man of thought
and the man of action is one and the same person, that the
Forms of the real world can ever be brought to birth in the
institutions of the familiar world. Herein lies the significance of
Plato's famous remark that man will never achieve salvation
or have surcease from misery, until philosophers are kings
and kings are philosophers.

There is a personal side to this recipe for salvation. Men
of thought—men that is to say who, in Plato's language,
know the Forms and spend their lives wholly in contemplation,
speculation and research—live less than the full human life
and fall short in their performance of the full human duty.

Socrates had taught, and Plato followed his teaching, that
the object of philosophy was not simply to obtain knowledge,
not even to obtain knowledge of the real world, but to acquire
something more precious than knowledge—namely, wisdom.
Now wisdom is knowledge in action; knowledge, that is to
say, applied to life. The application to life has a double
reference: first, knowledge can be used for the disciplining
of one's own desires and applied, therefore, to the leading of
the good life; secondly, knowledge can be utilized in the
service of one's society. And the two goals, the leading of the
good life and the helping of society, are not separate goals but
form the two halves of a unity. For man is a social being and
cannot come to his full stature and realize all that he has it
in him to be, except he live in contact with his fellows. Human
excellence, which involves the full development and right relationship of all the sides of our nature, is, therefore, essentially the excellence of a social creature, the excellence of the
citizen.

To produce this excellence is the object of statesmanship.

Hence the life of the philosopher and the life of the statesman are not, or rather they should not be, two different lives lived by two different kinds of men. The statesman ought to be also a philosopher and the philosopher a statesman; first, for the sake of the community, in order that, in the light of his knowledge of the Forms, the philosopher-statesman may so frame the laws of the State that the living of the good life becomes possible for every citizen according to his capacity; secondly, for the sake of the philosopher himself, that he may come to his full stature through the development of the social side of his nature in contact with his fellow-men in the conduct of affairs. To unite the philosopher and the statesman is thus at one and the same time to save society and to complete the philosopher. It is not, then, merely in repayment of the debt that he owes to the community that the philosopher returns to the Cave; he does so also for his own sake, in order that he may live out to the full extent of all his capacities and realize all the possibilities of his human nature.

Plato's Authoritarianism

The phrase used above, "the living of the good life . . . for every citizen according to his capacity", brings us to the charge against which I have still to defend Plato, the charge of Totalitarianism. For is there not, it may be asked, something familiar about this formula? Do we not know only too well the claim to regulate the lives of the citizens for "their own good"? Is it not precisely the claim that Fascism makes? In a formal sense it is, but the sense is only formal. What is important is the meaning which we give to the word "good", when we speak of "good" life.

Recipe for the Satisfaction of the Desires

In order that this meaning may be elucidated, let us return to Plato's divisions of the soul. The reasoning part, he insisted, should be in control of the others, not only in its own interests, in order that it might achieve a knowledge of reality unhampered by the solicitations of the spirited and the desiring parts, but also in *their* interests. Plato's view was that it is only when the third part of the soul is dominated by the first that it will thrive, even according to its own standards of thriving. What are these standards? The third part of the soul consists, it will be remembered, of desires and appetites, and for it the standard of success will, therefore, be found in the extent and frequency of their satisfaction. Now, if the appetites and desires are left to themselves, one of two things, Plato insists, will happen: either one desire will become a tyrant over all the rest and, in the interests of its own satisfaction, starve them of theirs; or each desire will claim satisfaction in turn, so that each in turn will dominate the personality.

The first case is that of the miser, the sensualist or the dictator—the tyrannic man, as Plato calls him. For the sake of gold, or sex, or power, these men live warped and mutilated lives, starving the rest of their natures in order to satisfy the cravings of the one master desire. Thus, the miser cannot afford to take his wife to the Riviera or even to the movies; the sensualist gives himself no chance to sample the possibilities of love; he is too busy pursuing his lusts; the power-lover, who uses people always as means—as means, that is to say, to the furtherance of his own ambition and never as ends—is a stranger to the joys of friendship.

The second case is the case of the man who, swept first by one impulse and then by another, is unable fully to satisfy any desire because before he has done so, he is called off by the solicitations of the next. Hence, he is precluded from the enjoyment of any full and lasting satisfaction. Plato concludes that it is only when the third part of the soul is in subjection to the rule of reason that its motley elements can achieve such satisfaction as is possible to them, since it is only when reason disciplines and dovetails the desires, rationing their various satisfactions according to the principle of justice, that each gets a fair deal. In a properly ordered soul no one desire is allowed to dominate the rest, or to prejudice the well-being of the whole, since, tamed by reason, the various desires have learnt to stand back and refrain from interfering with one another's satisfaction. Thus, the reasonable man, precisely because he is dominated by reason, is also a satisfied man. Plato transfers his conclusion from the stage of the soul to that of the State. Ordinary people, as we have seen, are those in whom the third part of the soul is predominant. Left to themselves, they are not capable of philosophy; they do not, that is to say, strive to know the principles of reality, they have little wisdom and are concerned only to satisfy their desires. It is for this reason that they crave money and power. The life of the ordinary man is, in Plato's view, at best a poor thing; he agrees with St. Paul that man is "born in sin" and with the writer of Ecclesiastes that his life is a succession of vanities. Tossed about on the sea of desire, the ordinary man is forever restless and discontented, unless he finds some positive reason for contentment. And so he tries to discover positive reasons, in women or in wine, in sport or in competitions, or even in war, and in pursuit of these will strive with his fellows. Such, too, is the condition of democracy, the condition of free competition, in which every man is as good as his neighbor (just as every desire in the third part of the soul is as good as its rival) and equally entitled with him both to govern and to be satisfied. Finding the resultant insecurity intolerable, democracies tend to develop into tyrannies, an absolute ruler being appointed to put an end to competition and party strife and to discipline the people for their own good and for the good of the community.

Plato's Account of the Power-loving Man and the Dictator State

The account of the transition from democracy to tyranny in the 8th Book of the *Republic* is a singular foreshadowing of the events which have taken place in Europe during the last twenty years. The disciplining of all for the good of the State sounds unimpeachable in theory and proclamation. But suppose that the so-called "good of the State" is only the good of the tyrant masquerading as the State! For what was the distinctive mark of the "tyrannic" man, as Plato calls him? He was the man in whom one tyrant desire for money, for sex or for power, has subjugated and disciplined all the others for the sake of *its,* not of *their* satisfaction. So, too, is it with the tyrant State.

The Nazi State and the Tyrant State

We are now in a position to indicate the lines upon which Plato would answer those who would criticize him for a Nazi authoritarianism. For the Nazi State is, it is obvious, not Plato's ideal State, but his tyrant State. In it there are two classes, the rulers and the slaves; but the ruling class rules not according to the dictates of reason, but for the satisfaction of desire; not of every desire, but of one tyrant desire that has subjugated all the rest. This is the desire for power.

"Wherever I found a living thing," wrote Nietzsche, from whom the Nazis derive some of their doctrines, "there found I the Will to Power; and even in the Will of the servant found I the Will to be master. Neither necessity, nor desire, but the love of power is the demon of mankind. You may give men everything possible—health, food, shelter, enjoyment—but they are and remain unhappy and capricious, for the demon waits and waits and must be satisfied."

Just as to the pursuit of this "demon" desire all other desires are subordinated, so, too, to the ambition of the power-loving class all other classes are subordinated. Just as the miser suppresses some of his faculties and harnesses others—for example, fortitude, endurance and self-denial—to the service of his master-desire, so the ruling class in the Fascist State suppresses recalcitrant individuals and subordinates the rest to its purposes, using them as raw material for the execution of its designs. Thus, we find the philosopher Fichte, one of the forerunners of Fascism, making a division of mankind into two classes of men—the noble man and the ignoble—who, as he says, "exists for the sake of the other" and "must likewise sacrifice himself". It is significant that the education of the ignoble must, according to Fichte, "consist essentially in this that it completely destroys freedom of the will".

If we ask how the noble are to be recognized, Fichte's answer is the same as Nietzsche's—by reference to their will to obtain and capacity for holding power.

If possession of power is the end and the will to obtain it the test of superiority, by what means, we must ask, is power obtained, and the possession of it, once it has been obtained, displayed? The answer is that it is obtained by the use of force and that its possession is displayed by domination over the wills of others. If there were no other men to strive against, power could not be obtained; if there were no other men to dominate, its pleasures could not be experienced nor its possession demonstrated. Thus, where power is the end, force is the means. It is the means by which the "good", power, is obtained, the means by which the "good", power, is exercised, and the test by which the possession of the "good", power, is demonstrated. For, where power is the "good", how is superiority in the matter of its possession to be shown, except by display of superior power? Or how can A show himself to be a *better* man than B, except by using more force and using it more successfully?

Unlimited and Dividing "Goods"

Plato makes an interesting distinction between those goods which are finite and those which are unlimited. Finite goods are those which are such that if A has them B cannot, since there is only a finite amount of the goods in question to go round; examples are money and power. Unlimited goods are such that the possession of them by A does not exclude the possession by B; examples are beauty and wisdom. The fact that I am enjoying a concert does not prevent—at least I hope it doesn't—B from enjoying it too; the circumstance of my acquiring a little wisdom does not prevent you from doing the same. It follows that, since in the tyrant State power is valued above all other goods and since power is a finite "good", there will be a struggle between rival claimants to obtain the largest share of it. Hence, the tyrant State will be always at war, open or disguised within itself.

Now let us compare with the tyrant State the structure of Plato's ideal State.

In this State the Guardians, in whom the reasoning part of the soul predominates, are the rulers. For them, there are two "goods", one intellectual, the knowledge and contemplation of the Forms; the other practical, the bringing of the Forms to birth in the structure, laws and life of the community. The mating of these two "goods" constitutes that wisdom which Plato held to be the highest excellence of man. For the others there is one "good", the gratification of their passions and the satisfaction of their desires in accordance with the discipline imposed by reason. Since they are unable to provide this discipline for themselves, it is prescribed for them by the scheme of education which the Guardians have drawn up for their training and the laws which they have framed for the regulation of their conduct. Since wisdom and knowledge are unlimited "goods", there is no competition among the Guardians for the largest share of them. The "goods" which the mass of the citizens desire are finite and limited, but the laws prescribed by the Guardians, expressive as they are of the principle of justice which operates throughout the State, whereby no one class meddles with the duties or privileges of the other two classes, are framed so as to ensure that for these limited "goods", the "goods" of the desiring part of the soul—wealth and comfort and gratified desire—there will be no strife of competition among the citizens.

Thus, whereas in the "tyrannic" State the object for which politics is conducted is power, power for the few over the many, in the Platonic State it is wisdom for the few and happiness for the many, happiness which, however, can be secured only if the many submit themselves to the guidance of the few. Plato's answer to the charge of authoritarianism is that men will enjoy a greater share of the "goods" appropriate to their natures—that is to say, happiness through the satisfaction of the appetites—under his system than they will do if they are free to govern themselves and follow their own desires. Hence, his endeavor to fix for all time the character of the ideal State.

Plato's Scepticism in Regard to Progress

Of human nature as a whole he took what we should regard as a pessimistic view, nor did he believe in what we call progress. The belief in progress in which most of us have been brought up would have seemed to him to be a by-product of certain accidental and particular circumstances —namely, the increased power over nature which, in the nineteenth century, enabled man to multiply commodities and to raise the material level of his life. By the aid of science men bade fair to subdue all their external enemies—fire and flood, pestilence, disease and want—and, encouraged by their success, they believed that by means of the extended application of science to human affairs, society would get better and better until Utopia was realized. This belief Plato would regard as a delusion. The real enemies of mankind are not pestilence or want or poverty, but man's uncontrolled passions and appetites. These, Plato would point out, have not been subdued by man's control over nature; they have only been given greater opportunities for gratification. Thus, the appetite for aggression has been sharpened by the increased powers of control and destruction which science has placed in the hands of dictators, while the motive of ambition has been strengthened by the prospect of gaining a new power over men's minds by capturing the modern instruments of education, the radio, advertisement and motion pictures. To conquer external nature is of no avail, while human nature remains unconquered; indeed, the conquest of nature is worse than useless, since it increases man's powers without increasing his wisdom in the use of them. It is for this reason that the progress of science has been accompanied by the retrogression of man.

Plato did not believe that the ordinary man was capable of improvement. Since, in him, the third part of the soul is in control, he will have no bridle to tame his passions, and no light to guide his steps. Therefore, he must be given guidance by others. Educated and guided by the wise and the good, he can be saved from the worst consequences of his wantonness and folly; but even the wisest legislation cannot improve his nature; it can only establish a form of society whose education is so devised, whose laws are so framed, and whose discipline is so tight that the passions of human nature are incapable of wrecking it. The object of politics, then, is primarily to protect the ordinary man from the worst results of his own passions. For the few, for those who are capable of knowing reality, its purpose is different. It is to be found in the achievement of certain states of mind which are good in themselves.[1] What is called morality, the right conduct of the individual life and its adjustment to the lives of others, and what is called politics, the right conduct of the affairs of the community and the regulation of man's social relationships, are, for Plato, simply means to the attainment of those states of mind that are good in themselves. If Plato is right, such states are realized only in the knowledge of reality. Hence, just as the railway system exists for an end other than itself, to transport people and commodities, so the social order exists in order that as many of those experiences which are good in themselves may be made available for as many as are capable of enjoying them. The ends of politics lie, therefore, for Plato, beyond politics and are to be found in the achievement of desirable states of mind by individual human beings. For the many, these desirable states of mind are comprised by the word happiness;

[1] See Chapter 5, pp. 127–132, for a development of the meaning of the phrase, "good in themselves".

for the few, they are to be found in the contemplation of the Forms, which constitute the world of value. Thus, the knowledge and enjoyment of value, known to us under the forms of happiness, justice, beauty, wisdom and truth is, for Plato, the object of statesmanship. I hope in the next three chapters to examine some of the conclusions which other philosophers have reached in regard to metaphysics, to ethics and to politics. In particular, I shall try to show to what extent they have followed Plato in postulating another order of reality, at once underlying and explaining the phenomena of the familiar world.

Chapter 4

THE ANALYSIS OF THE
FAMILIAR WORLD

The World of Common Sense

I DO not wish to suggest, as the conclusion of the last chapter may perhaps have done, that the revelation of values is the only, or even the main, object of philosophy. But it is one object and, since the student requires some thread to guide him through the mazes of philosophical speculation, the disclosure of values will, I hope, prove not less serviceable than another.

Forms, said Plato, alone are real, and among the Forms are what we call values; it follows that the familiar world of solid objects which we know by means of our senses is not wholly real. It will be the purpose of this chapter to try to summarize some of the reasons which subsequent philosophers have advanced on behalf of this conclusion. More precisely, since it is obvious that *something* we call the familiar world—the world that we know by means of our senses—exists and since it is difficult to see how a thing can exist and not be real, what we have to examine are a number of arguments which philosophers have advanced for supposing that its nature is very different from what in common sense we take it to be.

In common sense we take it to consist of a number of solid and liquid objects, some of them static, some moving about in space, and all of them consisting of what is called matter. Some of these objects we believe to be animated by minds, but beyond the presumption that mind is somehow different from the matter which it animates, common sense has very little to say about it. Besides being extended in space, the familiar world is also in time; the objects that belong to it have, that is to say, a history. Thus, the oak tree begins as an acorn, becomes a sapling, grows into a mature oak, decays and finally collapses. Yet throughout these changes it is taken for granted that the tree remains in some mysterious way one and the same oak tree. The oak tree, then, has a history, and to have a history means that you exist in time and remain the same thing throughout the changes that happen to you.

Now, the familiar world of things is known to us, at any rate primarily, through our senses; we see it, touch it, hear it, taste it and so on. If we had no senses, it may well be doubted whether we should know of the existence of the familiar world. Our knowledge, then, is, at any rate in part, derived from our senses. But does it all come from this source?

Empiricism and Rationalism

This question has provoked prolonged controversy; indeed it was upon it that in the seventeenth and eighteenth centuries philosophical discussion mainly centered. The controversy introduces the names of some celebrated philosophers. Those who maintained the view that, with certain qualifications, all our knowledge ultimately derives from the experience which reaches us through our senses are the English philosophers, Locke, Berkeley and Hume; they are called empiricists, from the Greek word *empeiria,* which means sense experience. Those who took the other side in this controversy are the French philosopher Descartes, the Dutch philosopher Spinoza and the German Leibniz. Broadly they held that the mind is fitted initially with certain faculties or principles of reasoning, and that if it reasons validly in accordance with these principles, it will reach true conclusions about the universe, including the familiar world. These philosophers are known collectively as rationalists, since they maintain that reason, operating in accordance with the laws of logic, can attain a knowledge of truths which owe nothing to sense experience. Knowledge obtained in this way is called *a priori* knowledge, since it is reached by the process of deducing something from a logically prior something else, which is taken to be true; more technically, it deduces conclusions from self-evident premises. Thus, when we deduce from the fact that a figure is a triangle that its three interior angles will be equal to two right angles, we have reached by the method of reasoning a piece of *a priori* knowledge.

Mathematics and logic are the two spheres to which the methods of the rationalists seem pre-eminently applicable. Thus, when I do sums in mental arithmetic, or discover that $(a^2-b^2)=(a+b)(a-b)$, my conclusions would seem to owe little, if anything, to sense experience. In denying that there can be knowledge other than that which comes to us initially through sense experience, the empiricists, so far at least as these two spheres are concerned, would seem to have been mistaken. On the other hand, the rationalists, in treating the universe as they did, as if it were a problem in mathematics, with the implied presumption that you could find out what was true about it by reasoning alone without having recourse at any stage to sense experience, would seem *prima facie* to have pushed the claims of reason too far. For there are some facts which, so far as one can see, can be discovered only by observation. Thus, no amount of reasoning will tell me that the moon's mean distance from the earth is 237,800 miles; that H_2O is the chemical analysis of water; or that there are 127 different kinds of wild flowers on the Sussex Downs. To discover such facts one must go and look; in other words, one must follow the method of science.

I cannot pursue this controversy; indeed, I have already been betrayed into writing of it at greater length than I had intended. I leave it here, permitting myself only to add that it comes to a head in the work of Kant, who is usually accounted the greatest of modern philosophers. Kant did not settle the controversy, but the effect of his work was to transfer the questions at issue to another plane of discussion, so that the empiricist–rationalist controversy has not, since his time, been pursued on the old lines. My present concern is with the philosophers' criticism of the familiar world of sense experience. Some parts of this criticism are derived from the arguments of the empiricists, others from those of the rationalists. I propose to say something about each of them in turn.

1. Empiricist Arguments against the Independent Reality of the Familiar World

Views of Locke

Locke maintained that what the mind actually knows when, as it believes, it perceives the external world, is its own ideas. Briefly his view was as follows: external objects impinge upon our sense organs and these stimulate the nerve endings—for example, in the fingers, at the retina of the eye, or in the ear-drums situated in the outer ears. As a result of this stimulation of the nerve endings, neural currents travel along the receptor nervous system into the brain, where they produce a complicated series of disturbances in the system of nerves which compose the brain. So far, we are in the realm of physiology, and most physiologists, I imagine, would accept our summary. But so long as we remain in this realm, the realm of purely *physical* happenings, consisting of movements of the pieces of matter which compose the nerves and the brain, there is no sensation and, therefore, no perceiving, for sensating and perceiving are events which take place in consciousness. Indeed, it is possible to suppose that all these physical happenings might have taken place exactly as they did, even if there were no mind to feel the sensations which normally accompany them. How, then, do the disturbances in the nerves which compose the brain produce an effect on the mind? How, in other words, do the events in the body and brain "get into" consciousness? This question raises the problem of the relation between the brain and the mind, a problem of which we do not know the solution. On Locke's view, the brain might be likened to a dark cabinet in which there is a lighted screen, the screen of consciousness. When the neural movements to which we have referred take place in the brain, there is thrown upon the lighted screen of consciousness a picture or representation of the external object whose impact upon the sense organs originally stimulated the series of neural happenings. It is this picture or representation that the mind knows. Hence Locke's view is often called Representationalism, since what the mind knows is, if Locke is right, not objects external to it, but pictures or representations of those objects thrown upon the screen of consciousness. These pictures or representations he called ideas.

Locke's view has two great advantages: it does, in the first place, make provision for the admitted facts that a complicated series of physiological events takes place in the body before we have the experience known as perceiving, and that the latest of these events in point of time occurs in the brain. In the second place, it enables us to understand why two people may have different perceptions of the same thing, as, for example, when I see green what a color-blind man sees gray, or I pronounce to be hot water which, to another man, seems tepid. These differences in the deliverances of our senses are readily intelligible, if in each case a different chain of neural machinery is set going by the stimulus of the same object resulting in different events in different brains and producing, therefore, in minds different representations of the object which acted as the original stimulus. It is because my body and brain are in a different condition from yours that, on this view, I have a different sensation of what we should both agree to be the same object.

But Locke's view is exposed to one objection which most people think fatal; this objection may be stated as follows. The view postulates three factors:

(1) the external object;
(2) the idea or representation in the mind;
(3) the mind.

Now, the mind, (3), knows the ideas, (2), but never knows the object, (1). Whenever it tries to do so, the ideas insist on intervening and getting known instead. How, then, the question may be asked, can the mind know anything about the object; how can it know that the object exists, and how, if it does exist, can it know that the object has the power of producing the ideas which are known? How, finally, can it know that the ideas are "like" the object in the sense of being pictures or representations of it? It would seem that Locke's theory of Representationalism effectively shuts out the mind from all direct contact with the outside world. Why, then, it may be asked, postulate an outside world at all?

This was the question which Locke's successor Berkeley did in fact put, and answered by eliminating the first factor, the outside world. Thus, Berkeley postulates two, and only two factors, in the process which we know as perception, the mind and the ideas which the mind knows.

Berkeley's Idealism

The student who is tackling philosophy for the first time can be confidently recommended to read Berkeley. Berkeley writes well and clearly and does not disdain the use of illustration which with him is both apt and copious; in fact in the abundance and appositeness of his examples, he excels all philosophers except Plato. In particular, I would recommend students to read the three dialogues between Hylas and Philonous which are printed at the end of the Everyman volume of Berkeley entitled *A New Theory of Vision and Other Writings*. In these dialogues Berkeley seeks to demonstrate the irrationality of believing in the existence of an external world of material things possessing fixed qualities and attributes. One by one he takes the qualities which we believe ourselves to perceive in the objects which are supposed to inhabit the familiar world and shows them to be relative to, and, therefore, dependent upon the perceiver. Here are a few of the more striking examples of the kind of consideration which Berkeley cites.

Heat, we should normally say, is a quality of the fire. I am standing, let us suppose, a foot away from it, and I say, "The fire is hot"; but if I gradually diminish my distance, my feeling of warmth gradually increases in intensity until it becomes a feeling of pain. Now, the pain is not in the fire, but in me; yet the pain is only a more intense degree of the heat; presumably, therefore, the heat was also in me. The fire, then, is not warm, it is only a something which has the capacity of producing a feeling of warmth in me.

Size, we should normally say, is a quality of things, yet size appears to vary according to the standpoint of observation and the nature of the observer's perceiving apparatus. For example, the size of a mite's foot is so tiny that I cannot see it; are we, then, to suppose that the mite is unable to see his own foot? This seems improbable.

Or take the case of texture; here is a surface which when I look at it with the naked eye seems to me to be smooth. But it has only to be observed through a microscope when it is seen to be covered with irregularities. (I refer the reader to the second satire of *Gulliver's Travels,* where little Gulliver is shocked to observe the craters, hillocks and forests which diversify the bodies of the Brobdignagian beauties whose smooth skins excited the admiration and provoked the sonnets of their gallants.)

Or take color; here is an object which appears to me to be green, or blue, or black, or gray, until I get jaundice or until somebody squeezes a drug called Santonin in my eyes, when it forthwith appears yellow. Take number; here is a lamp-post which to my normal vision appears single and solitary; but I have only to imbibe a sufficient quantity of alcohol, or to press my eyeball at the side with my finger, for it to become two. With what right, then, are we entitled to say that the object possesses some of these apparent qualities or attributes in its own right in some sense in which it does not possess any of the other apparent qualities and attributes? How can we ever know, in other words, that we are perceiving the object as it *really* is? If, however, we say that we are not perceiving an external object at all, but only knowing a set of ideas in our own minds, all these difficulties disappear.

The Evidence from Physics

The force of these considerations has been notably strengthened by the developments of modern science, with the result that a number of scientists have recently shown a marked disposition to flirt with idealist arguments and conclusions. The two sciences which are chiefly relevant to the issue we are discussing are physics and physiology. Physics shows that matter is ultimately analyzable into atoms, atoms which are divested of most of the qualities which common sense supposes matter to possess; such qualities as color, solidity, sound, smell, temperature are, in the physicists' world, simply not there.

Take, for example, the quality of heat. A gas, we are told, consists of molecules of about a hundred-millionth of an inch across, with comparatively large spaces between them, moving about in all directions with an average speed measured in hundreds of yards a second. The molecules meet and collide, and in consequence of their collision the gas has a certain temperature. If the gas is placed in a flame or hot body, the molecules of which it is composed will gain in energy, moving rapidly and colliding more violently. Gradually the temperature of the gas goes up; heat, as we say, is generated. But the cause of this heat is the greater energy of motion of the molecules; or, as a textbook on physics would put it, heat *is* nothing but the energy of motion of molecules.

Similarly, sound is said to be caused by, or alternatively to *be,* waves in the atmosphere. These waves vary in amplitude, in frequency of vibration, and in mode of vibration.

Variations in amplitude determine the loudness, in frequency of vibration the pitch, and in mode of vibration the quality of the sound. Sound, then, is produced by atmospheric waves. Atmospheric waves are described as regions of pressure and rarefication in the atmosphere moving forward with a certain velocity; and the movement of such regions of atmosphere is the cause of, or simply *is*, sound. For it is the properties of the atmospheric waves which the sounding body gives out which determine the character of the sounds which are heard.

Most significant of all is the case of color. Modern physics deals with immense numbers of electro-magnetic waves, which, so far as their intrinsic characteristics are concerned, differ from each other only in point of speed, wave-length and frequency. In terms of their wave-lengths and frequencies they are graded in the electro-magnetic spectrum. The rays which are called "light rays" occupy only a small part of this spectrum, at one end of which are located the so-called cosmic rays, and, at the other, wireless waves whose wave-length is measured in hundreds of yards. We may express this by saying that in the scale of wave-lengths and frequencies, according to which waves are arranged in the electro-magnetic spectrum, there is a certain section of waves which are—or which have effects which are—visible; these are called light waves.

Light, therefore, is, or is caused by, wave-lengths of frequencies falling within certain limits in the electro-magnetic spectrum. Within the section of wave-lengths which are, or which cause light, certain sub-sections are earmarked for the different colors. Thus, just as light waves constitute a section of the waves graded by the electro-magnetic spectrum, most of which are not visible, so each color is constituted by a sub-section of waves of particular frequency and wave-length falling within the light section.

But the waves in the light sub-section are not themselves colored.

I venture to remind the reader of the process whereby, for the purposes of illustration, we conceived ourselves to be stripping away the qualities of substance,[1] and then asked ourselves, what remains. Once again we put the question, what remains? It is difficult to say. In the nineteenth cen-

---

[1] See Chapter 3, pp. 40–41.

tury the answer would have been, solid, homogeneous atoms which move at different speeds and collide and combine in different patterns. The various qualities of the familiar world —its color, its sound, and so on—the nineteenth-century physicist would have said, are the result of the different patterns and forms of arrangement of colorless and soundless atoms. Just as the pieces of a jigsaw puzzle which are themselves without pattern, when correctly put together to make the puzzle result in a pattern which is colored and designed, so, it was believed, the atoms by virtue of their combination in different and varying patterns produce the colored design of the familiar changing world.

Idealist Tendencies of Physics

But for the homogeneous atoms of the nineteenth century, twentieth century physics has substituted positive and negative charges of electricity which are nevertheless not charges *in* anything, and other conceptions even more remote from the concepts of common sense. Now, if the apparently solid objects of the common sense world, each of which possesses a rich variety of qualities, turn out to be analyzable into quality-less charges of electricity, whence, it may be asked, do the qualities which we believe ourselves to perceive, derive? It seems difficult to resist the conclusion that they are contributed by the mind of the perceiver.

When the physicist falls in love, an event which must presumably on occasion happen to physicists, and feels impelled to kiss the girl he loves, does he, one wonders, *really* believe that those lips, rich, red, ripe, curved and soft, which offer themselves so sweetly to his own, are nothing but charges of electricity in motion and are, therefore, in their real nature neither rich, nor red, nor ripe, nor curved, nor soft? Of course he does not. Yet this, if he takes his physics seriously, is presumably what he ought to believe. Berkeley would tell him that the redness, softness and the rest were ideas in his mind—experiences, that is to say, or sensations of his own; yet I doubt if he would believe that either. Nevertheless, the conclusion of the argument—the conclusion, that is to say, which he *ought,* if he were logical, to accept—is that the familiar world outside him contains in its own right none of the qualities which he believes himself to perceive there. The conclusion has been put in a famous passage by Professor Whitehead: "Thus nature," he writes, "gets credit which should in truth be reserved for ourselves: the rose for its scent: the nightingale for his song: and the sun for his radiance. The poets are entirely mistaken; they should address their lyrics to themselves and should turn them into odes of self-congratulation on the excellency of the human mind. Nature is a dull affair, soundless, scentless, colorless; merely the hurrying of material, endlessly, meaninglessly." If the physicist believes this—as presumably he ought to do—some explanation should be forthcoming from him as to the reason for the presence in his experience of the qualities which, according to his analysis, are not there in the world outside him. None, however, is offered.

The Evidence from Physiology

The relevance of physiology is as follows. I have already referred to the machinery of perception and described how an external object impinging on one of the sense organs sets going complicated neural machinery which finally culminates in a disturbance of the nerve-cells in the brain. It is only *after* the disturbance in the brain has taken place that there ensues the psychological event which we describe as perceiving an object. But this account was deceptively simple. For how, we must now ask, *does* an external object impinge upon the sense organs? The answer is that the object, whatever the object may be, originates a chain of physical events which travel wave-like through the space intervening between it and our bodies, and that it is only when this journey has been completed that the sense organs are stimulated by the last of the events constituting the chain. Thus, in the case of visual perception, we see an object only when light waves, travelling from it at an ascertainable velocity, have reached the place occupied by the retinas of our eyes. In the case of aural perception, we hear a sound only after waves travelling through the atmosphere at a much smaller velocity have reached the drums which are situated in our outer ears. In the case of smell, we are made aware of the object which as we say, we smell, only when certain gases which are deemed to have been given off by the object from which the smell is said to originate, reach the nerve endings in our nostrils. I say gases, but, in point of fact, the stimulating agents are chemical substances which have to be dissolved in water before they are effective as agents of smell. Thus the immediate cause of the sensation we call smelling is a chemical substance dissolved in the moisture covering the nasal mucous membrane. Now the time taken by these various events—the journeying of waves in the electro-magnetic spectrum, the journeying of waves in the atmosphere, the journeying of chemical substances into the nostrils—is finite, though usually very short. Usually, but not always! Take, for example, the case of seeing a star. Astronomy tells us that from a certain area of space, thousands of millions of miles away, at a point in time which may have occurred several months ago, light rays emanated and proceeded to travel in all directions; these rays consist of complicated physical processes which, in common with all forms of light, are analyzable into waves in the electro-magnetic spectrum. Some of these rays reach the place where the atmosphere which envelops the earth begins. Here they are transformed into a different kind of physical process which, travelling through the atmosphere in the form of waves, ultimately penetrates to the place where our eyes are. Now, it is only after the waves have impinged upon the retinas of our eyes that the neural machinery which results in the events in the brain begins to function. Provided that it does function—provided, that is to say, that the end events take place in the brain—we shall experience the sensation which we call seeing the star. But all these processes have taken time; in point of fact, in the case which I have imagined, they have taken several months. During these months the star may have gone out of existence, or have changed into a different kind of star. Yet, provided the requisite events take place in the brain, we shall still have the sensation of seeing it. Now, we cannot, it is obvious, see a star that does not exist. We seem to be forced to the conclusion that whatever it is we believe ourselves to be seeing, what we see is certainly not the star.

What do we, in fact, see? A yellow patch of a certain size, shape and intensity which, by a series of inferences we connect with a star millions of miles away in space and some months ago in time; but these inferences may be mistaken. The patch may originate in a lamp hanging on the mast of a ship; it may have been due to a blow on the nose.

This, of course, is an extreme case, but it illustrates a principle which is applicable in all cases of visual perception since, however short the time which may be taken by the physical processes set going by the "object" in their journey to the place occupied by our sense organs, some time must elapse and during that time the physical object may in theory go out of existence. Yet, provided the events at the sense organs and in the brain occur, we shall still have the sensation of seeing it.

An analogous conclusion is reached by an examination of the machinery of hearing and touching. Take, for example, the case of touch.

I am, we will suppose, pressing my finger against the table, and as a result experiencing a sensation of coolness and hardness. Is this sensation caused by touching the table? Common sense says yes, but physics again says no. What happens, according to the physicist, is that electrical repulsion is developed between the atoms composing the finger and those composing the table. The harder I press the table, the stronger are the electrical forces which repel my finger. These electrical forces set up in the nerve cells at the end of my finger a current which reaches my brain, as the result of which I experience the sensation of touching the table. In fact, however, I am not in spatial contact with any object outside my body, and if appropriate parts of my nervous system are suitably stimulated, I shall experience the same sensation of touching the table, although there is no table to touch. What is more, I can experience what appears to be a sensation of a pin-prick in the non-existent finger of a hand which has been amputated, provided that the nerve terminals in my arm are suitably manipulated.

The conclusion of all these examples is the same; our bodies do not in sensation make direct contact with the physical object. We obtain information about it indirectly via the stimulation of our sense organs. Of what, then, it may be asked, do our senses make us aware, when we have sensory experience?

What is the Object of Immediate Sensory Experience?

This question could, it might be supposed, be answered by consulting the testimony of our own consciousness; it might also have been supposed that the answer would be unanimous. In fact, however, it takes us into a realm of controversy, and no agreed answer to it can be given. This is not only because different philosophers take different views of the nature of perception on the merits, as it were, of the case, but also because their views are influenced by their general metaphysical outlook within whose framework any theory of perception must be made to fit. Some philosophers have endeavored to maintain that we do actually perceive physical objects which exist independently of us, although they would, of course, admit that we only perceive parts of them: the outsides of apples and not their insides, the two near legs, the surface of the seat and the front side of the back of a chair, not the two hind legs, the under surface of the seat and the reverse side of the back. They also concede that the part we perceive and the aspect which the part we perceive will appear to us to wear will be determined by the position from which we observe it and by conditions prevailing in ourselves. Thus, I shall perceive a different part if I am a yard from the object, from that which I would perceive if my eyes were half an inch distant; the part I perceive will wear a different appearance if I have jaundice or am color blind, from what it would do if my health and my vision were normal, and so on. . . .

This view is the nearest to common sense which philosophers have found themselves able to maintain. Unfortunately there are many difficulties in it. Here are two.

The view presupposes that the object falls as it were into two parts, the part which is actually perceived and the part which is not perceived but which is, as it were, supplied by the mind on the evidence of what it does perceive. So far as the part which is actually perceived is concerned, the view would maintain that we perceive it more or less as it is, the presumption being that the object is lying out there in space waiting to be revealed to the mind which discovers it. How, then, it may be asked, are we to account for erroneous perception? Obviously we cannot perceive what is not there; when, therefore, we *seem* to perceive what is not there, as, for example, in the case of hallucination, or when the drunkard perceives a second lamp-post, or when the man with jaundice perceives a presumably non-existent yellow color, we must suppose that the activity of the mind is one of invention and not one of discovery. But if the mind can, on occasion, invent what it perceives, how can we distinguish the occasions on which it invents from those on which it discovers? The part invented seems to us, so far as its intrinsic characteristics are concerned, just as real as the part discovered. How, then, can we be sure that the mind has not invented the whole? Moreover, once we admit that the mind can invent or distort, how are we to distinguish erroneous from veridical perception? How can we be sure that the mind ever perceives anything exactly as it is? It might be said that we can appeal to the testimony of other people, but this resort unfortunately is closed to us, since once a doubt is cast upon reality of the objects we perceive, we can have no perceptual assurance of the existence of other people whose bodies are, after all, objects, perceived like other objects, whereby to substantiate cases of doubtful perception by us.

In the second place, we commonly assume that we perceive things as they are when we look at them from what might be called a regulation distance, say two or three feet, and have what is called normal vision. But why should they present a *true* appearance to eyes placed at a distance of a few feet and a false appearance to eyes looking from twenty yards, or to eyes looking through a telescope, or to eyes looking through a microscope, or to the eyes of a dog or of an earwig? The difficulty, then, which we are bringing against this view is that it offers us no standard by reference to which we can determine true and distinguish true from false perception.

The Sense-Data View of Perception

A second view maintains that what we are actually aware of when we have immediate sensory experience is what philosophers have called a sense-datum—that is to say, a something directly given to the senses.

A sense-datum is a patch of color, a rap of sound, a felt surface, or a smell. It is not the same as a physical object, nor is it identical with the surface of a physical object. Let us, for example, suppose that I am looking at a nickel and a quarter from a position which is considerably nearer to the nickel than it is to the quarter. When I look at the nickel, I shall see an elliptical silver patch; I shall see another when I look at the quarter. Now, the elliptical silver patch which I see when I look at the nickel will be larger than the one which I see when I look at the quarter; yet the quarter is larger than the nickel and both are circular. It follows that the two elliptical silver patches which I see cannot be identical with the surfaces of the nickel and the quarter. The two patches are examples of what philosophers call sense-data; they are usually supposed to be independent of my mind, though not necessarily of my body—what I actually see will, for example, depend in part upon the condition of my eyes and nervous system—and they constitute the objects of which my senses make me directly aware in sensation. The sense-datum theory of perception has in recent years been extensively discussed. One of the difficulties of the theory is the difficulty of determining the nature of the relation between the sense-datum and the physical object. No satisfactory account of this relation has been offered. If we say that the sense-datum is identical with or is part of the surface of the physical object, we encounter the difficulty that the sense-datum which I see varies with the conditions prevailing in me and also with the positions from which I am making my observation, whereas the object and, therefore, every part of the object, including that part of the object with which the sense-datum is supposed to be identical, is assumed to be independent of me and of the conditions under which I observe it. If, on the other hand, we say that sense-data and only sense-data exist in the outside world independently of me, and that the physical object is, as it were, supplied by the mind, we are driven to ask what are the rules according to which the mind does the "supplying" when, taking the sense-datum as a cue, it supplies the object. Why, in other words, when all that we actually see are brown patches, all that we actually feel, hard, cool surfaces, all that we actually hear, sharp, rapping sounds, do we supply table and not chair; and why, further, do the minds of all observers agree to supply table and not chair, although all the observers are, from the very nature of the case, experiencing slightly different sense-data? That they *are* experiencing slightly different sense-data follows from the fact that no two pairs of eyes can occupy identical positions at the same time, and the view of a "thing" from any one position is different from the view of it from any other, however close to each other the two positions may be.

A further difficulty is that the mind, when engaged in the process of "supplying", may make mistakes. If I go into a room in the dark, put out my hand and feel something soft and fluffy, I may conclude that it is the cat, or the hearth-rug, whereas it is, in fact, my wife's hair, my false conclusion being due to erroneous "supplying".

The questions which the sense-data theory must try to answer are, then, first, how am I to distinguish what I actually experience in sensation from what my mind supplies; and secondly, what do I mean when I say that my mind supplies wrongly? In the case of the last example I gave of the mind's "supplying", it would normally be said that it is my wife's hair that I am touching and not the cat or the hearth-rug; but if I never do and never can experience my wife's hair, but only sets of sense-data whose relation to the hair I am unable satisfactorily to determine, what ground have I for saying that this is what I do in fact touch? Indeed, what ground have I for postulating my wife's hair at all?

The difficulties in the sense-data theory suggest a third view which is substantially that of Berkeley.

The Idealist View of the Universe

This third view is that the status of the object which we know in sensation is mental, is, in fact, as Berkeley puts it, an idea in the mind of the person having the sensory experience. I do not propose to enter again into the arguments for this view. I confine myself to pointing out that it forms part, or can be developed to form part, of what is known as the idealist view of the universe. This view maintains that whatever exists, exists only by virtue of being relative to or dependent upon mind; or, as it is more usually put, relative to and dependent upon knowledge. It is inconceivable, say the idealists, that anything could be known to exist that is not an object of knowledge, simply because, in conceiving of it at all, we must conceive of it *as* an object of knowledge. We have no conception, then, of what a thing might be which is not an object of knowledge. Hence, the one quality which we can certainly predicate both of everything that we know to exist and of everything that we could know to exist, is that it should be a something known. Now, for a number of reasons, some of which have been given in the foregoing sketch of the theory of perception, it is held to be impossible for a thing to be an object of knowledge without being affected by the fact of being known. Thus, when I press my tongue against my teeth, what I am aware of is a feeling in my tongue; I am aware, that is to say, of a something which is unmistakably part of my psychology and would not and could not be what it is, unless I existed to have the feeling. When I am near the fire, what I feel is warmth—something that is again indubitably in me; when I stick a pin in my hand, what I am conscious of is a pricking sensation which may become painful, which once again is an occurrence in me. Similarly, the size of what we see depends upon our distance from it, and its color upon the condition of our visual apparatus; the texture of what we feel depends upon the degree of pressure which we exert and the sensitiveness or insensitiveness of our own skins; it also depends upon our temperature, one of the well-known effects of "having a temperature" which is above normal being that one feels things with a heightened sensibility. I do not, I repeat, propose to enter again into an account of these and similar considerations. Their upshot is in each case the same; whatever it is that we are conscious of in perception, this something is relative to and therefore in part dependent upon our consciousness for being the thing that it is; it is, therefore, affected by consciousness. Some philosophers have indeed maintained that the thing of which we are conscious is as truly a part of us as is our consciousness of it, being in fact a sensation, experience, or, as Berkeley puts it, an idea in our own minds.

Now, the idealist philosophy to which I referred above —it belongs mainly to the nineteenth century and is developed in detail in the works of Hegel and of the English philosopher F. H. Bradley—affirms that what is true of the object of sensory experience is true also of the object of knowledge; is, that is to say, true of the world we think about, no less than of the world which we perceive. And since the body is part of the world which we perceive, and since, therefore, the body and sense organs must, if the foregoing analysis be true, be accorded the status of ideas or sensations in the mind, the distinction between sensation and thought breaks down. Hence the attention of philosophers came in the nineteenth century to be concentrated less upon the problem of perception—how does a physical thing come to be perceived by a conscious mind when something stimulates the sense organs of the body?—and more upon problems of knowledge—what is the relation of the world which we know to the world as it is independently of our knowledge; how much does the mind contribute to the world which it knows and have we any ground for postulating a world which exists independently of our knowledge? The later developments of Idealism are thus concerned less with an analysis of sense experience and the relation of the mind to the physical world which sense experience is normally supposed to reveal, than with the functioning of the intellect and the immaterial worlds of logic and metaphysics which the mind explores. At this point we have passed insensibly as it were, as one so often does in philosophy, from the empiricists' criticism of the familiar world to the *a priori* arguments of the rationalists, who equally with the empiricists have denied that the familiar world is real and exists independently of ourselves. To these arguments, whose purport is that the general features which are supposed to characterize the external world are irrational and cannot, therefore, be accepted as real, we must now turn.

2. Rationalist Arguments against the Independent Reality of the Familiar World

(1) and (2) Substance and Change

At one of these arguments—the argument with regard to nature of substance—we have already glanced in the sketch given in the last chapter of Plato's Theory of Forms.[1] A common sense thing is normally supposed to consist of two factors, its qualities and the substance or stuff to which the qualities belong. But the qualities, we pointed out, are nothing in themselves or, more precisely, they are found continuously to vary, both in respect of their relation to the knowing mind and in respect of their relation to one another, while substance, bereft of its qualities, is again nothing or, if it is anything, it is that about which nothing can be said or known. The inference was that the familiar thing of the everyday world, consisting, as it is supposed to do, of substance plus qualities, cannot be wholly real. A similar treatment can be applied to the notion of change.

Things, we say, change; they have a history, growing, developing, falling away, and being dissolved again into their component elements, yet somehow contriving—so we nor-

---

[1] See Chapter 3, pp. 39–41.

mally suppose—through all these changes that happen to them to remain the same things. It is the same tennis ball that came from the makers full of air and covered with fluff as that which we discarded three years ago because the air had leaked or evaporated and because the cover had lost its fluff. Presently the children will get hold of it and knock it about, or the puppy will worry it; a hole will open in its surface, and the hole will become a slit along which it will ultimately be torn in two. But through all these changes, in spite of all these changes, it remains, we believe, the same tennis ball.

Similarly with psychological existents. Consider, for example, the case of a human being: I, we can say, am the man who when a baby aged three was dropped by his intoxicated nurse on the floor instead of into his cot; at the age of eight was chased by an angry market gardener out of his bean-patch; at the age of fourteen got a scholarship; at the age of seventeen and a half sprouted a moustache; at the age of twenty-one fell in love, and so on. Also, we can say, I am the man who will presently grow feeble in mind and decayed in body. One day this same man, who is I, will die. Now, not one of the molecules of my present body is the same as any one molecule of the body of the baby who was dropped by the nurse. Every scrap, then, of my material substance is different; so, too, are the qualities of that substance. The contents of my mind are also different—my capacities, propensities, faculties, tastes, as well as my sentiments, emotions, thoughts, memories and fears. Yet, we insist, I am the same person, albeit a changed person, as the baby was and the dying man will be. What follows? That the notion of a changing thing involves two factors. First, the changes that happen to it in virtue of which we say that it *is* changing and, secondly, an unchanging something to which they happen, a sort of core which remains unaffected by all the changes that occur in and to it. It is because of this core that we say that in spite of the changes it remains, nevertheless, the same thing. For if there were not this changeless core, there would be no *thing* to change; there would be only a series of changes which did not happen to any thing or in any thing. In order, then, that there may be a changing thing, there must be a continuing thread of identity along which the changes are, as it were, strung.

Now, the difficulty of the concept of change in its application to physical things is that no such continuing permanent core can be found. Not only are they changing all the time, but all of them is changing all the time. There is no single molecule of a thing of which it can be said that it is not in a continual state of change. For any thing that we like to choose—the tennis ball, for example—is, at any and every moment, further from the moment of its manufacture and nearer to that of its dissolution. If this is true of the tennis ball, it is true of every part of it. Of what, then, do we predicate the attribute of "sameness", when we say that it is the same tennis ball as it was yesterday and will be to-morrow? Do we merely mean that though it is substantially a different tennis ball, yet its appearance is so like that of the ball we saw yesterday that we call it the same for the sake of convenience? But if this *is* the explanation, it is not in the external world of substantial things that the continuing element of "sameness" is to be looked for, but rather in the world of Forms, using the word in Plato's sense, for it is the form not the matter which is the ground for the appearance of sameness. And it is because the appearances of the two balls are so alike that, for the sake of convenience, we talk and act as if the two appearances belonged to identically the same ball. But this suggestion is already taking us away from the common sense analysis of the physical thing and, if we were to develop its implications, as Aristotle, for example, does in his theory of Form and Matter, they result in a view very different from that of common sense.

Aristotle on Form, Substance and Change

Aristotle divided the objects of the familiar world into two elements, form and matter. The form of a thing is the sum total of all the qualities which it exhibits; the matter is that which has the form. Let us, in the light of this formula, consider an example of an apparently changing thing, a leaf which, we will suppose, is green in the spring and yellow in the autumn, and ask the question, what is it that is changed? The difficulty which the common sense view experiences in giving an answer to this question ought, I think, to rule it out of court from the beginning; for how can we say, as common sense does, that it is the *same* leaf when not only has every single molecule of which it is composed changed during the preceding six months but when every perceptible quality of the leaf—color, texture, size and whatever other qualities the leaf may possess—has also changed? If the common sense analysis is true, there is no ground for saying that it *is* the same leaf, precisely because no unchanging core can be found of which it can be said "although *this* which was green is now yellow, it has, nevertheless, somehow contrived to remain the same thing in spite of all the changes which have happened to it." Now let us consider the same example in the light of Aristotle's analysis. The matter, according to him, has not changed because, if it had, the leaf would not be the same leaf. What of the form? That has not changed either, since greenness cannot become yellowness. What in fact has happened is that one form, that of greenness, has been replaced by another in the same subject-matter; greenness has withdrawn and yellowness has taken its place. Thus, if Aristotle is right, no *thing* has changed; but if Aristotle is right, there is no *thing* which needs to change. The difficulty of the common sense view is that it both postulates a something to be the medium or the basis of change, while at the same time requiring it, just because it *is* the medium or basis of change, to be itself exempt from the changes that happen to it; yet the common sense view is totally unable to find such a something.

Now the physical world certainly *appears* to us to be a changing world; yet of these changes, it seems, we can give no intelligible account. What is the moral? There are many that might be drawn. One is that change is an illusion; a second that, as the philosopher Bergson maintained, change is the only reality; a third, that we have set ourselves an unanswerable problem by our initial presupposition that physical things consist of lumps of substantial matter with qualities tacked on to them—that is to say, by taking as real the familiar world of apparently solid and apparently changing things.

In this connection it is pertinent to note that psychological existents are not exposed to the same difficulty; at any rate in its application to them, the difficulty is less formidable. It may not be easy to determine in what sense I am today the same person as I was when I was a baby, but the notion of a continuing psychological identity does not affront the reason in the same way as the notion of a changeless, physical core. The conclusion is the same as that which we have already reached—the world that really exists must be other than the familiar world of material things which in common sense we take it to be.

(3), (4) and (5) Matter, Space and Time

As further examples of the rationalist criticism of the conceptions of the familiar world let us consider the notions of matter, space and time. Matter is extended—that is to say, it is spread out in and occupies space; it is also in time, possessing, as I have already explained, a history. Space and time are inalienable attributes of matter; we cannot, that is to say, conceive of a piece of matter which does not occupy space and—though the fact is not so immediately self-evident —we cannot conceive of matter which does not endure through time; for, given the assumption that the world consists of the familiar things postulated by common sense, then, just as one bit of a common sense thing will always be under or over or to the left or to the right of another, so one state or phase of it will always be before or after or simultaneous with another.

Philosophers have endeavored to show that this conception of matter is irrational, more particularly in regard to the spatial and temporal characteristics with which it is credited; but their arguments are not easy to state briefly nor is the conclusion which they are designed to establish always easy to grasp. The main argument, which I take from the philosopher Leibniz, runs as follows. Take a piece of matter, halve it and halve each of the resultant halves. The operation can, it is obvious, be performed indefinitely, nor is there any point at which the mind in performing it is brought to a stop. Matter, then, is infinitely divisible. But infinite divisibility, it is said, is an irrational characteristic because, as the mind proceeds with its halving operations, it demands some point at which it can halt, some *minimum divisible,* as it is called, at which it can come to rest and upon which it can rest. Now this it cannot find. But if there is no point at which it can come to rest, there is no "bottom" to matter, no non-divisible basis which can form, as it were, a solid foundation upon which the initial piece of matter which we began by halving can be built. Matter, in fact, under analysis dissolves into nothingness.

Again, assume the halving operation to be carried on until the mind reaches an infinitely small piece of matter. We must now suppose ourselves to be confronted with an infinite number of these infinitely small pieces or component parts into which our initial piece of matter has been broken; and we are trying, we will further suppose, from these parts to reconstruct the piece of matter with which we started. But having split up our initial piece of matter into an infinite number of infinitely small pieces, as we are certainly entitled to do, we discover that we can never put it together again, since one infinitely small piece added to another infinitely small piece still leaves us with an infinitely small piece. Now the piece of matter with which we started was conceived to have a finite size. Our difficulty is, then, that we cannot, from the collection of infinitely small pieces into which the finite piece of matter has been legitimately divided, reconstruct the finite piece of matter with which we started. The following quotation from Leibniz summarizes the conclusion of the argument which I have been trying to state. "It is impossible," says Leibniz, "to find the principle of a true unity in matter alone . . . since matter is only a collection or mass of parts to infinity." Not only is the finite piece of matter with which we started divisible to infinity, but it turns out to be without basis or foundation: ". . . every particle of matter," Leibniz continues, "is actually divided into other parts different among themselves. . . . And since this could always be continued, we should never reach anything of which we could say 'Here is a real being'."

Now there must somewhere be something which is ultimately real—something, that is to say, which resists endless disintegration under the process of analysis. If the foregoing argument is correct, it follows that this something cannot be a material lump occupying space, and the notion of matter as a candidate for the status of reality is accordingly dismissed as irrational. I have illustrated this conclusion by reference to the spatial characteristics of matter; a similar result could be reached by an examination of its temporal qualities.

(6) Relations

Another characteristic of the familiar world which has come under the fire of criticism is its "manyness". The familiar world contains a multitude of things which we take to be really different and separate from one another. We should, of course, agree that they influence one another in all sorts of ways—sun melting wax, east winds producing irritability, acid eating into metal and so on—but, we should add, in spite of this influencing, they nevertheless remain separate from one another, an influence being conceived as an emanation or force which originates in one of them, passes over the gap of "otherness" or "separateness" between them and "fetches up", as it were, on the other. If they were not separate, and, because separate, many, if there were not this gap of "otherness" between them, the apparent differences between them would be unreal and there would be not many things in the universe but only one.

It is precisely this—that the universe is not a multitude of different things but is a single whole or one—that many philosophers have maintained. Their view is called monistic, from the Greek word *monos,* which means "only" or "alone", and those who have maintained that reality is of this nature, is, that is to say, a single unity, are called "monists". The monistic view of the universe entails a distinction, famous in philosophy, between reality and appearance. For the universe does not appear to be a single whole or unity; on the contrary, the universe appears to consist of a vast number of separate, independent things. According, however, to the contentions of the monists, this appearance is fallacious, being due to the partial or limited character of man's vision. If I could enlarge my vision, this appearance would, they maintain, be seen to require correction, and I should see as the related parts of a single unified whole what now appear to me as a number of separate and unrelated entities. Hegel's philosophy seeks to show how, by following a particular philosophical method, the partial vision of my separate, finite mind can be corrected and enlarged. One example of this method is the monists' treatment of relations. These, according to the monists, are not, as they appear to be, separate and distinct from the things they relate, but form together with them an integrated whole. Everything, the monists point out, is given to us enmeshed in a network of relations. If it is removed from this network of relations and considered by itself, as for theoretical purposes it undoubtedly can be, it is no longer the same thing.

Take, for example, the case of a potato. What do we know about it that we can put into words? That it is more oval than a billiard ball and softer than a stone; that it requires less sunlight to grow than is needed by a tomato plant; that it can be planted in the early spring and dug up in September; that potatoes multiply in the earth and that as many as a dozen potatoes may be found growing on the same root; that when put into a basket with a number of other potatoes and taken to market it will sell at 10¢ a pound and so on. Now each of these statements that I have made about the potato involves a reference to something else, its purport being to state the potato's relation to that something else. Furthermore, all these things that I have said are true of the potato only because it *has* these relations to other things; if it did not have them, the statements would not be true of it, and if they were not true of it, it would not be the potato that it in fact is. Therefore, its relations to other things play an integral part in making it what it is, and apart from them it would not be what it is. Hence, a thing's relations to other things are just as truly parts of it as are its qualities; they are also, by the same argument, just as truly parts of the other things to which it is related. Thus, it and the things to which it is related are parts of one another or, more precisely, they form together a single whole such that, to abstract any element, whether thing or relation, from the whole, and to treat it as if it existed in and by itself as a separate thing, is to falsify it. Common sense makes this abstraction and so does science; hence they give us false pictures of reality, since the entities which they treat as real have, in fact, been torn out of the context of relations in which they are initially given and in which, therefore, alone they are real. If a thing is real only in the context of the environment in which it is given and to which it belongs—if, in other words, it is real only as part of a larger whole—the same consideration applies, it is obvious, to the larger whole. This also is real only as part of a whole yet larger than the first whole and belongs to it as its part. The application of the argument can be extended indefinitely until it brings us to the whole which includes all the others, the whole of wholes. This is nothing less than the universe. The conclusion of the argument is that the universe, which is the whole of all the other wholes, is alone fully real. Everything else falls short of full reality precisely because, since it is less than the whole of reality, it must, if considered by itself, as science and common sense consider it, be taken out of the context of those relations to the rest of reality which help to constitute its full being. Two metaphysical conclusions follow. First, the differences between things are not wholly real; hence reality is not many but one. Secondly, things by themselves are not fully real; they are only aspects of the whole of reality which expresses itself in them. At best they are partially real and, if they are taken as being wholly real, real, that is to say, as entities subsisting in their own right, they are misleading as well.

The Scientists' Accounts of Personality

The foregoing argument has been abstruse, and the conclusion in which it issues is repugnant to twentieth-century common sense, which under the influence of science is instinctively disposed to take as its standard of reality pieces of matter existing in their own right and extended in space. It is a world so constituted that science explores, and we have grown up to accept the findings of science both as true and as final. The theory that we have just been considering denies these findings. It affirms, first, that the pieces of matter taken by themselves are not quite real, since they are abstracted from the context of the larger reality in which they occur; the conclusions of science are therefore, it insists, not quite true. It affirms, secondly, that they are not really separate from other pieces of matter but are aspects of a single whole or unity which expresses itself in them and determines their nature. Hence it establishes a different conception of what "to be real" means from that accepted by common sense.

A positive example may perhaps serve to illustrate this conception; the example is a human personality. Now of a human personality as a whole science can give no account; if it tries, all that it succeeds in telling us about are the various parts or aspects of the personality. Of these various parts the different sciences have much to tell us. Indeed, each separate aspect of a human being is assigned to a special science, and of this aspect the relevant science purports to give a reasonably full account. We will suppose that these various accounts are drawn up and collated. We will imagine ourselves to begin with the physiological account in terms of organs, tubes and pipes, nerves and bones and blood vessels. These, presumably, can be analyzed into their chemical constituents, and there is, therefore, a chemist's account in terms of molecules and elements. These, again, can be analyzed in terms of their atomic constituents, and to the chemist's, therefore, we must add the physicist's account in terms of protons and electrons.

Beginning at the other end of the scale, we shall have to include the psychologist's account in terms of mental events, images, sensations and so forth, with special departmental accounts such as the behaviorist's in terms of language habits and conditioned reflexes, and the psychoanalyst's in terms of unconscious desires and promptings of the libido. From other points of view there is economic man and there is the median man of the statistician; there is man from the standpoint of the biologist and man as he appears to the anthropologist. Each of these accounts could in theory be made accurate and complete—complete, that is to say, so far as it goes; yet each would be couched in different terms. To say that no one of these accounts conveys the whole truth about a man, but describes only some particular aspect of him which has been selected for special attention, would be to state a commonplace.

But we can go further. Let us suppose that all the different accounts—the physiological, the chemical, the physical, the psychological, the behavioristic, the psychoanalytic, the economic, the statistical, the biological and the anthropological—were rendered complete, collated, supplemented with other accurate but partial accounts and worked up into a comprehensive survey; they would still fail to constitute *the* truth about a man. And they would fail to do this, not because some particular piece of information had been left out, or some particular point of view forgotten—for no matter how complete the collection of scientific accounts might be, the truth would still elude them—but because they would remain only a set of separate accounts of different parts or aspects, and a man is more than the different parts or aspects which are ingredients of him. True knowledge of a man is not, in other words, the sum-total of the complete and accurate accounts of all his different aspects, even if those accounts could be made exhaustive. True knowledge is, or at least includes, knowledge of the man as a whole.

By what method, then, can a human being be known as a personality? First, imaginatively, by the method of art. The great novelist or playwright who, as we say, knows the human heart can create characters as large as life, through whom we obtain an insight into human nature which, unassisted by his deeper vision, would have been denied to us. Secondly, intuitively, by acquaintance and more fully by affection; the way to know persons is to live with them; the way to know them best is to love them. Here, then, is a kind of knowledge which science cannot give us; moreover, it exhibits the kind of knowledge which science does give us—knowledge of glands, or blood pressure, or complexes, or emotional disposition, or type of imagery—as being knowledge of a series of parts or abstractions from the total human being that the friend or lover knows. Now what matters about a man or a woman as a man or a woman, is not any of the things that science tells us, but what sort of person he or she is; for it is in this, in his or her personality, that his or her reality consists.

In the second place, the personality as a whole is not made up of parts but is prior to them, expressing itself in them and known or divined through them. Here is a man whose eyes are bright; the corners of his lips turn up; his complexion is fresh; his step alert; his gait springy; his handclasp firm; when he meets you, he looks you straight in the eyes. A successful happy man, you divine, sure of himself, in control of himself and his life, one who knows what he wants and is confident of his ability to get it, yet—and here we note the kindness of his eyes—one who will not ride roughshod over his fellows in ruthless pursuit of his own interests.

Here is another man whose eye is dull and fishlike; his step is listless; his hand flaccid and his grasp nerveless; his cheeks sag, the corners of his mouth droop; a failure, we say, one in whom the flame of life burns low; not interested very much in anybody, perhaps not even in himself; or perhaps he is a hypochondriac, wrapped up in his own diseases, obsessed by his own grievances, a nervous little clod of wants and ailments, perpetually grumbling at the universe because it will not organize itself with a view to making him happy.

These, of course, are crude examples; inevitably, since I am no delineator of character. But the novelist or the playwright could elaborate my crude character sketches in an infinity of different ways, asking me, for example, to observe the wide spreading nostrils of the dramatic orator or the long upper lip of the professional comedian. Now in each of these cases the personality is divined from the bodily appearance and behavior, the word "behavior" covering the speech, of the person. We say that his personality expresses itself in his behavior; we observe that by dint of so expressing itself, it has gradually moulded the medium of its expression so that under the perpetual stress of disappointment and disillusion the corners of the mouth of "the failure" begin gradually to turn down.

The personality, then, is more than the sum of its parts and expresses itself in them. It is also *prior* to its organs of expression, in the sense that it moulds and shapes them, making them what they are, as when we say that the eyes are the windows of the soul, or that the happy disposition *informs* the smile. This is the reverse of the ordinary arithmetical method of computation, according to which we say that the parts come together or are added together to make the whole.

Now the philosophical theory of Monism asks us to conceive of reality as a whole which expresses itself in the everyday things and also in the individual persons who confront us in the familiar world, just as the personality expresses itself in the stance or the gait of a man's body, in the cast of his features or in the turn of his expression, each of which is only a partial expression of the whole man who unifies them all, and not after the model of separate, isolated pieces of matter lying about in space, divided by gulfs of real difference from other bits and existing in their own right unconnected by any unifying principle.

Retrospect and Conclusions

In this chapter I have been engaged in sketching a number of philosophical conclusions and summarizing some of the arguments by which they are supported. The arguments have one feature in common: they are all hostile to and, if successful, destructive of the familiar world, and the positions which they are designed to support all represent the universe as being in reality very different from what it is assumed to be by common sense.

The arguments have fallen broadly into two groups. First, the arguments of the empiricists, starting from an examination of the reports of sense experience, sought to show that the world to which our senses introduce us is not, as it appears to be, independent of our experience of it but is, at least in part, dependent upon, even if it is not wholly constituted by, the minds which know it. Secondly, the arguments of the rationalists subjected a number of the familiar features of the everyday world—change and substance and "manyness"—to investigation and convicted them of inability to sustain the weight of critical analysis. What, in fact, the rationalists have endeavored to show is that, if these supposed features of the familiar world are taken as real, then the mind in the course of examining them is led into contradiction precisely because they are themselves contradictory concepts.

I also followed one of the paths which, assuming the validity of rationalist criticisms, philosophers have traced from the given world consisting apparently of many individual things extended in space to a reality which is a single whole or unity expressing itself in the infinite variety of the familiar world. In so doing, I went beyond my brief, which in this chapter, was designed to cover only the philosophers' criticism of the familiar world. The departure was, however, at least in part deliberate, since it paves the way to the next stage in the philosophers' journey which is the endeavor to establish the *positive* nature of reality.

For something, it is obvious, must be real, and if, accepting for the moment the negative criticisms of this chapter, we agree that this something is not the familiar world, we are driven to look for it elsewhere.

In the last chapter I sketched Plato's conception of reality as a system of immaterial Forms. My own view is that Plato's conception is correct in so far as it asserts that, when we are looking for an examplar for reality, we are nearest the mark when we identify it with what the modern world calls "values". The most manifest examples of the values are truth, goodness and beauty, which may be conceived after the model which Plato established for the Forms. It may, of course, be the case—theologians say that it is the case—that these values are only the expressions of something more ultimate still, being in fact the modes under which an infinite personality, whom we worship as God, reveals himself to mankind. (At the end of the next chapter reasons will be given for thinking that the value of goodness at any rate may most appropriately be so conceived.) Moreover, any philosophical view, such as that which we have been considering in the immediately preceding pages, which insists that the world is a unity must issue in a similar conclusion, in that it will regard each of the values as a partial expression of the immanent whole which is the universe. I cannot further follow these speculations in the present book, but must confine myself in the remaining chapters to the attempt to reveal values as the underlying realities both of ethics and of politics. We have briefly considered some of the arguments which seek to establish the existence of an immaterial reality underlying the familiar world; we will now extend our examination to the moral consciousness of man and to the principles which underlie the policies of States.

Chapter 5

ETHICAL PHILOSOPHY

The Common Sense Attitude to Ethics

THE common sense attitude to the familiar world tends to deny that there is any reality other than the reality of the things which I see, touch, hear, smell or taste. That is to say, it tends to deny the existence of an order of reality which is not open to the investigation and subject to the laws of science. There is an equivalent "common sense" attitude to human conduct; this tends to deny that anything in the psychological realm is real other than the series of emotions, desires, impulses, hopes and thoughts which make up the stream of my consciousness. Its effect is, therefore, to deny that there can be any motive to action other than the solicitations of our desires, wishes and impulses. When what I have called the "common sense" attitude to conduct meets with the apparent fact of moral obligation, which forces itself upon us most strikingly in the familiar opposition expressed in the phrase, "I want to do this but I *ought* to do that", which I thereupon proceed to do in spite of my very manifest desire for "this", it regards the compulsion signified by the word "ought" as a rationalization of disguised desires or concealed fears.

I say that this type of view in regard to ethics has affinity with the "common sense" view in regard to metaphysics because, like it, it tends to deny the presence in the universe of values which exist in their own right and which human consciousness can recognize as the ends of human conduct and the goals of human aspiration, as what, in fact, we commonly know as ideals. Just as in metaphysics the common sense attitude reduces the familiar world to the province of science, so in ethics the common sense attitude reduces the human soul to the province of psychology. If common sense is right, physics and psychology could, provided that they were sufficiently extended in scope, tell us all that there is to be known about the universe, since, on this view, there are no realms or orders of being other than those which physicists and psychologists explore.

By analyzing the process known as perception, I sought in the last chapter to show the inadequacy of this attitude and summarized some philosophical views which have maintained that our inventory of the universe must include factors or elements other than the world of apparently solid, common sense objects. In this chapter I shall try to show the inadequacy of the equivalent "common sense" account of the facts of human experience in the sphere of ethics, the implied conclusion being that an order of being other than the psychologists' world of thoughts, desires and emotions, must be postulated in ethics just as an order of reality other than the physicists' world of matter in space must be postulated in metaphysics. To this conclusion most ethical philosophers have subscribed.

But let us first see in a little more detail to what the common sense analysis of the facts with which ethics deals amounts.

1. Subjectivist and Naturalist Theories of Ethics

The Objective View of Ethics

When I say "this is right" or "this is good", I should normally be supposed to be making a statement about the nature of "this", asserting that it is characterized by the quality of rightness or goodness, just as, when I say "the fire-box is red", I should normally be taken to assert that the fire-box is characterized by the quality of redness. It would follow from this, the normal view, that if I thought that "this" had the quality of rightness when it had not, or failed to recognize in "this" the quality when "this" in fact possessed it, I should be making a mistake, just as I make a mistake when I think that three and two make seven, or even that the temperature of a room is 70° when the thermometer shows it to be 67°, or when I think that the train is due to leave at 7:50 when it is, in fact, due to leave at 7:45. It will also follow from what I have called the normal view that some people—those, namely, who habitually make fewer mistakes in these matters than others—may be credited with the possession of a well-developed and sensitive moral sense, that is to say, a power of discernment or insight, in virtue of which they are enabled to detect the presence of ethical qualities when they are, in fact, present and are not led falsely to suppose them to be present when they are, in fact, absent. Ethical theories of this type are called "objective" because they assert that there is an "object", an institution, it may be, or a person's character, or a course of conduct, or a particular action which possesses ethical qualities in its own right, with the corollary that there can be correct ethical judgments, that is to say, judgments which rightly recognize and affirm the presence of such qualities.

Subjectivist Theories. What they Assert

Now, the subjectivist theories of ethics do not accept this view. Let us call the person making an ethical judgment the subject, and the institution, character or course of conduct to which the judgment refers the object. The subjectivists maintain that ethical judgments do not refer to the object to which they purport to refer but do in fact refer to the subject, being judgments to the effect that the subject is experiencing certain feelings or entertaining certain opinions. Thus they translate "this is right" into "I am experiencing an emotion of approval for this", and proceed to give as the reason why I experience this emotion my belief that "this" will conduce to my advantage. It follows that if these theories are correct, "this" has no ethical quality in its own right; I project on to it a quality which it has not, in fact, got because it arouses a feeling of approval in me. It follows further:

(i) That there can be no differences of opinions about ethical matters, since, if I say "this is right" and you say "this is wrong", we are not making two contradictory ethical judgments about the same thing, one of which is correct and the other incorrect; each of us is passing a judgment about something different, I asserting that the emotion aroused in me is one of approval, and you that the emotion aroused in you is one of disapproval. Hence, unless we are deliberately lying, our two judgments, though they appear to contradict one another, do not, in fact, do so and both can be correct.

(ii) That to speak of a developed moral sense or a sound ethical judgment is meaningless. Since an ethical judgment consists, on this view, in asserting merely that our feelings or opinions in regard to something are so and so, the only sense in which one so-called ethical judgment can be more correct than another is the sense in which A may be a better observer of his own feelings than B.

Such theories are also called "naturalist" or "naturalistic" theories, because they proceed on the assumption that the natural world of which our minds with their emotions, desires and so on form part is the only world, and that it is not necessary in explaining ethical experience to postulate any order of reality other than the natural world. This is in fact the view which most common sense people seem disposed to take when they make acquaintance with philosophical ethics for the first time, though it is not the view upon which they habitually proceed when they pass the moral judgments of everyday life.

Psychological Origin of Ethical Sentiments

I have so far only described subjectivist or naturalist theories; we must now consider the grounds on which such theories are put forward. This can most conveniently be done by considering rather more closely the *reasons* for the feelings of approval and disapproval into which what appear to be ethical judgments about the goodness or badness of things, people, institutions and so on are analyzed. These feelings are explained by a reference to their origins. A certain course of action, we will suppose, has been found by me over a long period to produce advantageous consequences. It has made me comfortable, or great, or powerful, or famous, or wealthy, or has resulted in the enjoyment of agreeable sensations. Consequently, I approve of this course of action and call it good. Such are the bare bones of the theory; in the course of development, however, it grows more complex and becomes very plausible. For example, we can say that the course of action in question was found by my ancestors over a long period to be productive of satisfactory consequences; that, in consequence, this and similar courses of action have for centuries won the approval of my ancestors, and that as a result I am born with an inherited disposition—"an instinct" psychologists would call it—to approve of this course of action without reflecting upon or without even being aware of the reasons which originally led to the approval being felt. It is on these lines that subjectivists analyze the moral sense, the faculty which, known popularly as "conscience," figures so largely in ethical discussion and experience. In so far as the explanation is valid, it is obvious that it applies to feelings of disapproval no less than to feelings of approval. In fact, it applies more markedly, since it is in feelings of disapproval that conscience chiefly manifests itself. Thus my conscience may strongly disapprove of incest, and if I commit it or feel tempted to commit it, I shall suffer from feelings of guilt and remorse. If asked why I feel guilty, I should find it difficult to answer. There is nothing obviously painful, or ugly, or wicked about having intercourse with one's sister, nor, we are told, does incest produce results which are biologically deleterious in the possible offspring.

The theory which we are examining would, however, find little difficulty in providing me with an answer. Early societies, it would point out, are ridden with prohibitions and taboos. A common taboo relates to intercourse with those members of the tribe who are closely related to oneself. Why? There may be a number of reasons; for example, exogamy, marrying outside the tribe, may evoke a disposition to military aggressiveness in young males who are forced to seek their brides abroad while, at the same time, reserving a surplus of females for the enjoyment of the old-man rulers. An alternative view which has been suggested is that the existence of a taboo upon intercourse between nearly related males and females would have the effect of diminishing the occasions for jealousy and strife within the tribe; it might also reduce the incentive for young males to question or resent the authority of the old-man ruler or rulers.[1] Most authorities seem, in general, to be agreed that the incest taboo is the offspring of tradition rather than the expression of instinct, and there seems to be little evidence for the view that, at any rate in the short run, incest leads to biological deterioration. (It is not, of course, suggested that savage tribes *reasoned* in this way; merely that, if these theories which I have taken from writers on anthropology are correct, those tribes which practiced incest would show a tendency to grow weaker through

---

[1] These and other interesting speculations are taken from J. J. Atkinson's work *Social Origins and Primal Law.*

internecine strife or long-run biological deterioration and to die out, while on "survival-of-the-fittest" principles those which placed a taboo upon marriage with one's near relations survived and prospered.) Whatever the reason which originally led to the prohibition of intercourse within certain forbidden categories—and we may be sure it was a good utilitarian reason—the fact that it *was* prohibited, and continued to be so for centuries, has resulted in an inherited instinct of repulsion in the modern civilized descendants of the savage tribes which tabooed it, an instinct which lies at the root of the feeling of moral guilt.

Recent writers on psychoanalysis have, of course, enormously extended the scope of this kind of interpretation by referring the origin of feelings of guilt to the traces left in the unconscious self of forgotten events in early childhood or even, on some extreme theories, in the womb. This is not the place for a discussion of the Oedipus Complex, the relations between the super-ego, the ego and the id, or of other psychoanalytical conceptions. It suffices to point out their bearing upon subjectivist modes of explanation, which is that, in so far as they are valid, they tend to resolve what appear to be ethical feelings of guilt, remorse and even conscientious disapproval into non-ethical origins, the memory of which, being painful, has been repressed into the unconscious, but which presently find expression in conscious manifestations which we mistakenly take to be genuine ethical judgments. Thus, I think that I genuinely disapprove on grounds of ethical good taste of young people making public love in the passages of the London tubes. These things, I say, *ought* to be done in private. Why do I think that they ought? Because, it may be—and I am here illustrating rather than endorsing the psychoanalytic view—of certain improper advances made to me as a little boy of three by an inquisitive or lascivious nurse.

Social and Economic Origins of Ethical Sentiments

Or we may vary our explanation by giving greater weight to the influence of society. Here, let us suppose, is a nomadic, tribal community in constant danger from more powerful neighbors. What are the qualities in its members which will best conduce to its survival? Courage and loyalty in men to defend the tribe, and connubial fidelity and chastity in women to keep up its numbers, the best recipe for the production of children being not one woman and many men but one woman and one man. These qualities are accordingly encouraged while the reverse qualities are punished with disapprobation, flogging and in extreme cases death, with the result that centuries later we honor heroes and give them the Victoria Cross, admire the "old-school-tie" spirit in public-school men—with what uncritical loyalty it inspires them to rally round, when the traditions or welfare of the sacred institutions which have made them what they are, are threatened—and visit with social ostracism the woman who loves out of wedlock, while branding her children as bastards. The conclusion of this line of thought is the same. I approve or disapprove now, without knowing why I do so, of courses of conduct and qualities of character which the early community from which mine has developed approved and disapproved, because they respectively conduced to or militated against the safety and welfare of that community.

A variant of this account emphasizes the *class* structure of society.

All societies that have ever existed, it points out, have been based on the government of the many by the few, who have used their power to exploit the many in their own interest. The lives of most people who have ever lived have as a result been meagre, wretched and oppressed. As slaves, or serfs, or wage-slaves, they have toiled to fill the bellies or line the pockets of idle lords and masters. Or they have provided them in the shape of fighting men with the raw material upon which their ambitions for glory, dominion and power were fed. What has induced the many to put up with this treatment? Force, no doubt, but not only force; for the moral sentiments have been recruited in force's assistance, the rulers having throughout history made the laws, laid down the lines of education, and set the standards of public opinion including, therefore, those of right and wrong, to operate in their own interests. The consequence is that by mere dint of obeying the laws and of accepting the standards, the many conduce to the maintenance of the power of the few. Our ethical notions, then, are the prop of our rulers' power. We are animated by those moral sentiments, we accept those standards of valuation which will automatically conduce to the welfare not of society as a whole but of the governing class of society. This line of thought is first suggested by Thrasymachus in the first book of Plato's *Republic,* where he defines Justice, by which he means social morality, as "the interest of the stronger". It is further exemplified by Lenin's indictment of religion as "the opium of the people". Indeed, the whole philosophy of Marxism endorses and develops this treatment of ethics. There are, it maintains, no absolute rights and wrongs; there are only those rules, codes, judgments, sentiments and valuations which reflect the needs and interests of the dominant class in the community. Thus, there are *bourgeois* justice and *bourgeois* morality; there are also, or rather there will be also, proletarian justice and proletarian morality.

Bourgeois morality receives its most striking exemplification in the laws for the protection of private property. Why were poachers savagely flogged? Why was the laborer who stole a sheep to feed his starving family transported for life? Why, even today, does the man who beats his wife black and blue get a shorter sentence than the man who poaches a salmon out of a Scottish river? Because of the strength of the sentiments which are evoked by property. It is in his ownership of property that the superiority of the *bourgeois* consists and upon it that his power depends. Therefore, whatever contributes to its preservation is good; whatever threatens it is evil, while the advocate of Communism is denounced as an agitator whose pernicious doctrines threaten hearth, home, family tradition, morality, religion and whatever else is noble and sacred. Proletarian morality is exemplified by Prudhon's succinct statement, "Property is theft".

But it is not necessary to be a Marxist, the argument continues, to perceive the origins of the most refined moral sentiments in considerations of economic utility. Why, for example, has sexual morality always been the special concern of women? Why are women so much more severe upon erring sisters than men upon wild-oat-sowing brothers? Because for centuries the only way in which a woman could maintain herself was by leasing the use of her body to a man. She could lease it to one man for life—profession of wife—or to a number of men for short periods—profession of prostitute. The wife and the prostitute have historically constituted the two women's Trade Unions, and the free lover who gave for nothing what other women were only prepared to give for "keeps" was denounced impartially by both as a traitor whose behavior cut at the very roots of women's livelihood.

Herein is to be found the origin of women's concern with

the proprieties. But the origin of the sense of propriety is very different from its content. The nice women or, more precisely, the nice women of my youth, were quite genuinely shocked by sexual laxity, in ignorance of the origins of and the reasons for the feelings of shocked disgust by which they were so deliciously agitated.

Though they are economic and utilitarian in origin, moral sentiments have, as Marx pointed out, a life of their own. They may, that is to say, persist long after the economic or social needs from which they took their rise and from which they derived their justification. Thus, the institution of monogamy, which, according to the view we are considering, originated in the need for an expanding population coupled with the importance of avoiding internal rivalry and strife between the many claimants for the more desirable woman, obviously demanded for its smooth working a substantial equality of numbers between the sexes. In England in the first decade between the two wars there was a surplus of some two million women. Nevertheless monogamy persisted, and departures from the code which it sanctioned were officially regarded as social misdemeanors, even though, in fact, they became increasingly frequent and, while still deplored, were reprobated less severely than in the past. Assuming, however, that this account of the origin and nature of moral judgments is correct, then if the surplus of women continued we should be entitled to expect a modification of the laws relating to monogamy; we should also expect the modification to be accompanied or succeeded by a change in moral sentiments, so that for a rich man to have two wives in Balham would occasion no more moral perturbation than it does in Mecca or Baghdad. Meanwhile, it is instructive to note that since many women have become self-supporting, divorce has become easier, more frequent and less reprobated than in the days of women's complete economic dependence, while in Nazi Germany the State's need for children to maintain the supply of *Herrenvolk* led to the unmarried mother receiving State bonuses instead of black looks.

Reasons for the Variety of Moral Judgments

All these illustrations may be used to exemplify the same general conclusion, which is that our moral judgments do not relate to, or pronounce upon the ethical characteristics of the object, whether the object is a person's character, a course of conduct, a code or a set of institutions, to which they purport to refer. For objects, on this view, have no ethical characteristics. Hence ethical judgments and sentiments are simply rationalizations of the needs and wishes either of the person judging, or of the society to which he belongs. They report, then, not upon the nature of the thing judged about but upon the condition of the subject, and they have no more validity than the smoker's belief that tobacco ash is good for the carpet, or the fisherman's that fish, being cold-blooded, do not mind having their throats torn out of them by a hook; to adopt a modern term, their status is that of "wish fulfilments".

It is only on this basis, we are told, that we can explain the otherwise bewildering variety of man's moral judgments. For if an object X is really characterized in its own right by an ethical quality E, it is hard to believe that human beings should have differed so widely in their views as to whether E was present in X or not; it is also hard to believe that they should have attributed the same ethical quality E to so many widely different characters, qualities and actions according to the age, time and place in which they have happened to have lived and the class into which they have happened to be born, holding, if they are born in a bedroom in Balham in 1918, that there is one God, that Jesus Christ is His Son, that they ought to marry one wife, that private enterprise is salutary, property sacrosanct and Germans wicked; if in a bedroom in Baghdad, that there is one God, that Mohammed is his Prophet and that it is right to marry as many wives as one can afford to keep; if in a bedroom in Moscow, that private enterprise is inefficient, that property is anti-social and that Germans, who were comparatively virtuous in 1940, became wicked in 1941. To quote a well-known authority on ethical philosophy, Canon Rashdall:

"There is hardly a vice or a crime (according to our own moral standard) which has not at some time or other in some circumstances been looked upon as a moral and religious duty. Stealing was accounted virtuous for the young Spartan and among the Indian cast of Thugs. In the ancient world Piracy, *i.e.*, robbery and murder, was a respectable profession. To the Mediaeval Christian religious persecution was the highest of duties, and so on."

Now what more plausible explanation of these divergencies could there be than that which attributes them to different needs and circumstances in the persons or communities responsible for making the divergent judgments and valuations? These, it is said, do not, then, report of an object X that it has the character E; what they do report is the fact that the subject S is experiencing a certain need, is moved by a certain desire, has inherited a certain tradition or is anxious to gain a certain advantage; and since the need, desire, tradition and advantage vary, so do the ethical judgments which rationalize them.

Subjectivist Theories Congenial to the Age

Through the many variations of this view runs a common factor. In respect of this factor the view is analogous to the common sense and scientific analysis of the familiar world; that is to say, it denies the existence and influence upon the natural world of any non-natural order of reality. When it seeks to explain the phenomena of the natural world, it attributes them always to natural causes.

I do not, of course, mean that ordinary decent people deny that there are such things as ethical qualities and characters; deny that A is a "crook" and B a "decent chap" and that it means something to say that they are, or deny that so-and-so is our duty and ought to be done whatever the consequences may be. On the contrary, most people's experience does undoubtedly contain what seem to them to be *bona-fide* ethical elements, and they would be frankly and rightly appalled if asked to accept the explanation at which I have just glanced which derives these ethical elements from non-ethical origins. But these, it might be said, are people who are not accustomed to analyzing their experiences; they are content to take them at their face value.

What I do mean is that Naturalism and Subjectivism are embedded in the climate of our age, a climate which has largely been formed by science; that most people, accordingly, when they think about these matters for the first time, take kindly to the naturalist and subjectivist mode of explanation of which examples have been given, a mode of explanation which insists that what I have called the "face value" of ethical experience is misleading (it is an odd thing, by the way, that the equivalent interpretation of the external world in idealist terms—ethical subjectivism says this is good = this arouses a feeling of approval in me, while subjective idealism says this is red = this arouses a sensation of redness in me—is rejected almost as invariably as ethical subjectivism is embraced), that many people who have dabbled in philosophy never pass beyond this mode of explanation, but rest content with it until the end of their days, and that it shares with the common sense and scientific explanations of the familiar world the characteristic of postulating no order of reality other than the familiar world. Just as science is content with a world of matter in motion, so subjectivist ethics is content with a world of human consciousness which contains nothing but the stream of desires, impulses and events which psychologists catalogue. The former rejects the notion of an immaterial reality which underlies and explains the phenomena of the world of matter in motion; the latter rejects the notion of a moral order which gives meaning and significance to ethical judgments. What can be urged against this view?

2. Objectivist Theories of Ethics

(A) Criticism of Subjectivism and Naturalism

Of the many criticisms of the view that I have been engaged in sketching I will select five, which must for reasons of space be shortly summarized.

(1) What is Right Contrasted with what is Thought Right

The argument from the variety of moral notions does not prove what it is invoked to prove. What it proves is that men's notions of right and wrong differ enormously. It also shows that these notions are influenced by all manner of subjectivist considerations, personal, social and economic. What it does *not* prove is that right and wrong are themselves subjective in the sense of being influenced, or even determined by these considerations. Let me cite an analogy which will serve to bring out the point at issue. Let us suppose that two people, who have just entered a room, are asked to guess its temperature; the one, we will suppose, has recently emerged from a refrigerator, the other from a hot-house; the former guesses 75° F., the latter 70° F. It is clear that the subjective conditions prevailing in the bodies of the two judgers have deter-

mined the guesses that they make as to the temperature of
the room; what they do not determine is the temperature of
the room. What both judgers are purporting to assess is a
certain condition which prevails in the world independently
of their judgments, and most of us would agree that, since the
temperature of the room can be measured by a thermometer,
there is a perfectly definite sense in which the judgment to
the effect that it is so and so would be objective and right,
while another judgment to the effect that it is something else
would be objective and wrong; moreover, one judgment would
also be said to be nearer the truth than another.

In exactly the same way the fact that men have historically
differed about what things are right and what things are
wrong does not mean that there is not an objective right and
an objective wrong about which they are taking different
views; nor does it mean that some of these different views
may not be nearer the truth than others. The difference between the two classes of case, the case in which we judge
about the temperature and the case in which we judge about
ethical qualities, is that in the former we can refer to an
instrument, the thermometer, by reference to which we can
determine what the objective temperature is and pronounce
one judgment to be nearer the truth than the other, whereas
there is no equivalent instrument wherewith to measure ethical
judgments. But the fact that we have no means of telling with
certainty which of two ethical judgments approximates more
closely to the truth does not mean that there is no truth for
them to approximate to. Nor does it mean that one of them
may not approximate more closely than the other.

In point of fact, there is among almost all men a general
consensus of opinion in regard to certain general ethical
principles, as, for example, that kindness is better than cruelty,
honesty than deceit, truth-telling than hypocrisy, though there
is wide difference of opinion about the application of these
principles to particular cases. It may also be noted that the
ethical precepts of all the great religions tend to converge, in
proportion as these religions embody developed spiritual experience. The rites of the Aztecs may differ widely from
those of the Druids, but the injunctions of Buddha and Lao
Tse on the subject, for example, of resisting evil not with a
contrary evil but with good, are very similar to those of Jesus
Christ. Thus, the deliverances of man's moral sense are like

a pyramid; starting at the bottom from widely spread bases, they tend to converge at the top.

All this admittedly does not show that ethical judgments are objective. What it does do is to show that the particular argument for believing them to be subjective, which is derived from the variety of man's ethical judgments, is fallacious. The argument applies not to what is right, but to what is thought right. It is only if we take the view that the two concepts, what is right and what is thought right, mean in the last resort the same thing, that the argument proves what it purports to prove. But whether they do or do not mean the same is precisely the point at issue. The argument, then, not only begs the question, but steals the answer.

(2) The Argument from Origins

Part of the subjectivist case rests upon what is known as the argument from origins. This maintains, in effect, that ethics arises from a non-ethical origin, man's opinions about right and wrong having developed by traceable stages from primitive prohibitions, such as are exemplified by tribal ritual and taboo; "this", in fact, is thought right by me today because centuries ago something like "this" was found to be advantageous by the primitive community from which my community has developed. This argument, it will be remembered, was applied with special force to the development of conscience.

Let us assume for a moment that what it asserts is historically correct and that ethics has, in fact, developed from non-ethical origins. Why should it be assumed that there is no more in ethics now than there was in the origins from which it took its rise? If we take the notion of development seriously, there is obviously more in the developed product than there was in its origin; more in the oak than in the acorn, more in the mind of Einstein than in that of a baby, more in the spiritual consciousness of a saint than in the superstitious fears of the savage. Moreover, the "more" may involve a difference in kind, as when from the association of two elements, oxygen and hydrogen, we get a developed product water, which is different from either of them and contains qualities, such as that of wetness, which is not in either of them. Or, consider the parallel case of mathematics; nobody would argue that the fact that the savage can count only upon the fingers of one hand in some way throws doubt upon the validity of the multiplication table.

Assuming for a moment that there is more in the developed product than there was in the origins, can we give any account of this "more"? Yes we can, by looking towards the end whose realization is the goal of the developing thing. This goal may be the achievement of the condition which constitutes the full development proper to its species as in the case of the perfect specimen of the fruit, the vegetable or the tree, or it may be something external to itself, as, for example, in the case of the ideal to which a human mind aspires, the realization of this ideal being, as the Greeks would say, the "good" of the developing mind. If we take this line, we shall add with Plato and Aristotle that it is not until it realizes its fullest development, not until it achieves its "good", that the thing becomes fully itself. Take, for example, the case of a growing human being. I am, we will suppose, a visitor from Mars, asking to be shown a specimen of the human beings who, I have been led to understand, inhabit the planet called Earth. What sort of specimen am I to be shown as an example of the type? An embryo? Obviously not; nor a baby; nor a boy; nor even a youth. Why not? Because all these, we should say, are undeveloped; are, therefore, lacking in respect of some of the attributes which belong to fully developed human beings. Neither the embryo, nor the baby, nor the boy, nor the youth, has fully realized the potentialities of his human nature. In order, therefore, that I may fully comprehend the sort of being that a man is, I must, it is obvious, be shown a specimen of the species at the height of his powers with all his faculties developed and all the latent potentialities of his nature unfolded. It does not matter, from the point of view of the argument, what stage we choose to exemplify this state of full development—I personally am apt to place it later than I used to do—but it is clear that, whatever the stage may be, it is only in so far as it is reached that the "nature" of human beings can be understood, precisely because it is only in so far as it is reached that the nature of human beings is exemplified. What is the implication? That there is in a fully developed man, more than there was in the embryo or the baby; that to understand that "more" we must know what is the particular kind of end or goal at which the human being's development is aiming, the implication being that even if the end or goal is never fully realized, it is only in the degree of an individual's approximation to it that the character of the species to which the individual belongs can be fully understood.

The same conclusion holds in regard to the development of man's ethical consciousness. It follows that to demonstrate that man's ethical consciousness had humble beginnings, or that it developed from non-ethical sentiments and impulses, does not show that it may not be something very different from these sentiments and impulses now. In particular, it may be genuinely ethical now even if in its origin it was not.

(3) The Distinction between "Right" and "Pleasant"

But can we accept the view that ethical consciousness did develop from non-ethical origins? What sort of origins may we suppose them to have been? They are presumably to be found in considerations of expediency. According to the theory under discussion, I approve of "this" because, in the long run, "this" turns out to my advantage; or of pleasantness—I approve of "this" because "this" gives me pleasure. Now, expediency and pleasantness turn out, on analysis, to be the same. For what do we mean by saying that so-and-so is to my advantage? Conceivably that it brings me money or power. Why do I want money? Because of the things that money will buy. Champagne, for example, or a Rolls Royce. Why do I want champagne? Because the drinking of champagne gives me agreeable sensations. Why do I want a Rolls Royce? Because it runs smoothly—more agreeable sensations—or because it enables me to show off before the neighbors—agreeable emotions—or because it helps me to travel sooner to my objective, in order that I may the more rapidly transact my business, in order that I may make more money or make it more quickly, in order, then, that in making and subsequently in spending the money I may enjoy more agreeable sensations—or because it gives me a sense of power. And why do I want power? Because its possession is intrinsically satisfying, or because it enables me to order people about, or to impose my will on others, which ordering and imposing are again accompanied by or are the source of agreeable sensations and emotions. Thus, the concept of expediency resolves itself on analysis into the concept of pleasure. Indeed, once we take the significance out of morality by adopting a subjectivist view of ethics, it is exceedingly difficult to resist the reduction of all human motives to the one motive constituted by the desire to obtain pleasure for the agent.

This reduction is frequently made. A celebrated psychological analysis seeks to maintain that the only possible object of human desire is pleasure and this analysis is the basis of a well-known ethical theory, known as Psychological Hedonism.

I cannot here describe this view at length,[1] although I shall refer to it again later in the Chapter.[2]

In point of fact, however, the process of analysis upon which I have just been engaged affords a good indication of the way in which the hedonist position may be supported. Adopting for the moment, for the purposes of argument, the view that motives of expediency do resolve themselves in the last resort into the desire to obtain pleasure for the agent, we may restate the subjectivist position, "I hold this course of conduct to be right and approve of it, because either now or in the past the consequences of following it have brought me, or the community to which I belong, pleasure."

(4) That the Concepts of "Right" and "Ought" are Unexplained

One objection to this view can be put very simply. We are all, in practice, accustomed to the familiar distinction between "right" and "pleasant". "This," we say, "is what I should like to do, but that is what I ought to do." Thus, "I should like to take my girl to the movies, but I ought to stop at home and look after my aged mother", or "to read for my examination", or "to put a new washer on the faucet . . ."; "I should like to turn a dishonest penny by buying and selling on the Black Market, but I know that it would be unpatriotic and dishonest to do so"; "I should like to divert suspicion from myself for this murder or this theft by incriminating my friend, whom I believe to be innocent, but I know that it would be wrong to do so, even if I yield to temptation and do it". This distinction between "want" and "ought", between "pleasure" and "right" is, I repeat, very familiar. How, then, if the view which I am engaged in criticizing is valid, did this distinction come to be made? If to say "X is right", means, in the long run, no more than to say "X gives pleasure", why did we go out of our way to invent a

[1] I have endeavored to do so in my *Guide to the Philosophy of Morals and Politics*, Chapter 11.   [2] See pp. 133–136.

meaningless conception, that of "right", in order deliberately to set it in opposition to the meaningful conceptions of "pleasure" and "self-interest"? How, indeed, *could* we have done so, if in the long run the meaning of "right" is precisely the same as that of "pleasure" or "self-interest", seeing that, if it *is* the same, no opposition between them can, in fact, arise? (When I distinguish between A and B, the fact that I do so implies that there are distinguishable differences between them. I cannot distinguish between A and A.)

Nor does it help matters to say, as the subjectivist is apt to do, that there is in fact a distinction—the distinction, namely, between short-term pleasure to me and long-term advantage to the community. Thus courage, the subjectivist might say, may entail short-term pain for the brave man, but long-term advantage for his community whose safety is ensured by the bravery of its citizens, and, he would add, safety is valued because in the long run it brings pleasure to the community and so in the long run to the brave man, as a member of it. Hence, it comes about that the community praises courage as a good, condemns cowardice as a vice and so on. . . . I have been through this analysis before, and need not repeat it here. For this defense, if it were in fact to be made, does not really save the subjectivist position, since it is based upon an opposition between short-term personal pleasure and long-term social advantage. But what, we must ask, *is* long-term social advantage? The use of the phrase in this connection can only mean one or other of two things, either:

    (1) That a man can be influenced by genuinely altruistic considerations, or

    (2) That as a member of the community which has been saved and caused to prosper by the quality of courage which he has exhibited he will presently enjoy pleasure, *e.g.*, the pleasures of a good reputation, a pension and the Victoria Cross.

If it means (1), the implication is that a man can be influenced by moral considerations which are not analyzable into expectations of pleasure; if it means (2), then the opposition is between short- and long-term pleasure for the man who faces the dangerous situation. If this is all that the opposition does mean, why should we not say so? Why, that is to say, should we go out of our way to invent what is, on this view, a totally meaningless conception—namely, the conception of morality—and say "right", when what we mean is "long-term pleasure"? Why not say simply to the man we are exhorting to be brave, "Running away will mean some pleasure for you now, but steadfastness will mean more pleasure for you and for the other members of your community in the long run"?

Our difficulty, then, is this; if there is no unique meaning for the word "right", if, that is to say, the meaning of the word can always be analyzed into considerations of pleasure and advantage, whether short- or long-term, how did "right" ever come to be distinguished from pleasure and advantage? At this point we pass from the criticism of Subjectivism to the statement of an objective theory of ethics.

(B) Statement of Objectivist Ethical Theory
Kant's Negative Moral Theory. Man's Character as Determined

Emphasis on this distinction—the distinction, namely, between "right" or duty on the one hand and personal pleasure or advantage on the other—lies at the basis of one of the best known theories of morals, that of the philosopher Kant. In his analysis of human impulses and desires, Kant went all the way with the subjectivists and the naturalists; indeed, he went further, showing how what we desire and value is always determined for us by forces and factors over which we have no control. Study a human being scientifically and you will find it difficult to avoid the conclusion that Kant is right. For each of the sciences shows us the human being as determined by a different set of considerations. Thus biology presents us with man as a member of a particular species endowed with the desires, instincts and traits appropriate to that species. Anthropology exhibits him as a member of a particular cultural group with the tastes, preferences, prejudices and modes of valuation natural to the group; I, for example, am a child of the twentieth century, with the beliefs, tastes, attitudes, habits, likings and dislikings appropriate to a middle-class Englishman who is also a citizen of a country which at the time of writing is engaged in a life-and-death struggle with Nazi Germany. Physiology and psychology combine to exhibit me as the end product of a complex series of factors and influences which determine my bodily and mental constitution. For example, I have received certain combinations of genes from my parents which determine my bodily and—many would add—my mental make-up. I have been placed and have grown up in a particular environment, made up of family, school, acquaintances, friends, traditions, with which this inherited physical and psychological make-up of mine reacts, these reactions contributing in their turn to train and develop what I am pleased to call my character. For the initial inheritance of bodily genes and potential character traits which constitute the stock in trade I bring with me into the world, I am not responsible—not responsible, for example, for the fact that I dislike marzipan, like asparagus, feel giddy on heights, am comparatively unappreciative of poetry, and will sell my soul for music. Further, I am not responsible for the environment in which I am placed and grow up; therefore, I am not responsible for the character which results from the interaction of the two. And because I am not responsible, I cannot properly be praised or blamed. Thus, the fact that I have no temptation to drunkenness or sodomy is no more a cause of self-congratulation than my tendencies to irritability and selfishness are matters for reprobation, since I am no more accountable for the so-called good in me than for the so-called bad. All this and more Kant fully admits. Take me purely as a creature of likes and dislikes, of wants and needs, of impulses and tastes, of preferences and prejudices, and it is difficult to avoid the conclusion that I am merely a by-product of the influences and forces which have made me what I am, reflecting them as completely as a plant reflects the nature of the seed from which it has sprung, the qualities of the soil in which it has grown and the peculiarities of the climate to which it has been exposed.

The Unique Significance of "Ought"

So far we have considered man purely as an inhabitant of the natural sphere, the sphere in which we find and treat a human being as we might find and treat any other natural phenomenon—that is to say, as a being completely determined by the raw material of its initial inheritance and the conditions of its environment. But, says Kant, we have left one characteristic possessed by this purely natural phenomenon out of account. It is a characteristic unique in nature, and man, by virtue of his possession of it, cannot be adequately regarded as wholly a child of nature. The characteristic is this, that in addition to the impulses and desires which tell me what I would like to do, I am, on occasion, conscious of something else—namely, of what I ought to do. And what I ought to do may be different from, indeed, it may be the very opposite of what I would like to do. Thus, for man, and for man alone among the inhabitants of the natural world, there is a distinction between "want" and "ought", between desire and duty.

The distinction means that when we have completed our analysis of all the factors in a man which are due to his inherited psychological and physiological dispositions, to his race, his class, his environment and his training—of all the factors, in short, as the result of which we feel entitled to say, "Yes, considering his antecedents and his home, taking into account the way he has been brought up and the bad company he has got into, we can quite understand that *this* is the way he naturally would behave"—when, I say, we have done all this, we can always go on to add, "But *that*, nevertheless, is the way in which he ought to have behaved," and in saying this we are implying that he always could have behaved as he ought to have done. For to say "you ought to have done so-and-so" when we know as a matter of fact that you could not have done it, makes nonsense. Nobody says that a stone *ought* to roll uphill, or that a tiger *ought* not to tear its prey, because we know perfectly well that, given the nature of stones and tigers, they could not act otherwise than they do. We understand, that is to say, that they are wholly determined by their nature and their circumstances.

In applying, then, the term "ought" to a man's conduct, we are implying that he has a sense of moral obligation and we are implying further that, in virtue of his possession of that sense, he is free—free, that is to say, from determination by natural circumstances, free to do his duty. As Kant puts it, "ought implies can". What is the corollary? That in respect of his moral sense man escapes the network of influences and antecedents that determine the rest of his nature and that, in so far as he is able to perceive the path of duty and free to follow it, he is not a purely natural phenomenon. For whence, Kant asks, could this sense of "ought" be derived? One method of accounting for it, the method of deriving it from non-ethical origins in the past, I have already glanced at, cit-

ing some examples of this mode of explanation in the sketch
of subjectivist ethics given in Section A above. Briefly, this
account ran as follows:

(i) Men did certain actions in the past.

(ii) They found that these actions had undesirable consequences, either personal or social, and, if social, then
also personal, because the community punished the individual for performing actions harmful to it.

(iii) Therefore, when our ancestors performed these
actions, they had a feeling of apprehension lest they be
found out and punished.

(iv) Their descendants inherited the feeling but forgot
the considerations which had led to its formation.

(v) Therefore the descendants have an inherited sense
that certain actions are wrong and ought not to be done
because they are wrong.

I have briefly glanced at some of the objections to this
view. The main and immediately relevant objection is that
it fails to account for the uniqueness of the conviction "I
ought not" and the feeling of guilt that is associated with it.
What, if the subjectivist explanation is correct, we should
expect, is a distinction between short-term satisfaction and
long-term dissatisfaction. For example, we should expect
someone to say, "I want to enjoy the woman now because I
shall derive intense sensual satisfaction from doing so; but I
shall probably be found out and ostracized, perhaps even
assaulted by the woman's husband; or the woman will become
an emotional or a financial burden. These consequences will
be extremely unpleasant. Therefore in the end the long-term
undesirable results of enjoying her will exceed the short-term
desirable results; therefore, as a sensible man, I will decide
on balance not to."

These, as I say, or something like these, are the sentiments and considerations which, if the subjectivist view
were correct, one would expect to pass through a man's
mind when considering whether to make love to his neighbor's wife. They may be expressed by the familiar opposition
"I want X but don't want the consequences of X", an opposition which makes use of one counter and one only, the
counter of "want" or "need". But this familiar opposition
does not do justice to the psychological experience of the

moral opposition between "I want to do X because it is pleasant, but I ought not to do X because it is wrong", not, be it noted, "because in the long run X will bring unpleasant consequences." Indeed, one may feel that X will be pleasant both in the short run and in the long and think no undesirable consequences need be anticipated from doing it; and yet one may also feel convinced that one ought not to do it. Whence, then, does this sense of moral obligation, with its attendant emotion of moral guilt, derive?

Kant's Positive Theory of Morals

Kant's answer is that since its origin cannot be found in the world of nature, that is to say, in the familiar world of matter which physics studies and analyzes, or of living organisms whose evolution biology and, in the case of the living organism known as man, anthropology traces, we must look for it elsewhere. Everything in nature, he points out, acts as it does because it is made as it is; and, being so made, it can do no other. This, too, as we have seen, is true of man, in so far as we can consider man as a purely natural phenomenon; he follows his instincts, gives way to his impulses and satisfies his desires because it is his nature so to do and his instincts, impulses and desires are those appropriate to his nature. In so far, then, as a man ever does something which is other than what he wants to do—wants, that is to say, in the long run, when all the consequences both of doing it and of not doing it have been taken into account —he does this "something other" for a reason unconnected with fear of consequences; when, in short, he recognizes his duty and wills to do it irrespective of whether he wants to do it or not and irrespective also of whether he actually does do it or not, then, in respect of his experience in so recognizing and willing, he must, Kant insists, be a member of some other order of reality. In virtue of his membership of this other order he can win free from the influences of heredity, circumstance and environment which otherwise determine his psychology, just as in virtue of his membership of that order he is removed from the sphere of the spatio-temporal influences which determine his body. In respect, therefore, of his ability to act as a moral agent, acknowledging the pull of duty and exerting his will to do it, he is free or, more precisely, he is determined only by himself; that is to say, by his own recognition of a moral order which exists in the universe, and to which, precisely because his real self is a member of that order, he owes allegiance.

This may seem to be a formidable theory to account for the peculiarly compulsive feeling with which the notion of "ought" comes to us. Indeed, taken by itself it cannot but seem arbitrary. To see it in its proper setting, we must associate Kant's moral with his metaphysical theory.

Kant's Metaphysical Theory

Briefly the conclusion of Kant's metaphysical theory is that the world we know by means of our senses, equally with the world about which we think, when, for example, we use our reasons to reach conclusions, are worlds which our own minds have in large part constructed. In sensing and thinking, then, we make contact, only with a world which is dependent on us. It is the world as it appears to us, rather than the world as it is. I cannot here enter into an account of the reasons for this conclusion. I mention it only because it throws into relief the special significance of the conclusion of Kant's moral theory, according to which, when we encounter an experience which is recognizably moral, as, for example, when we will to do our duty in the face of disinclination, we are making direct contact not with the world which "appears" to our senses and is in part constructed by our intellects, but with the world as it is independently of ourselves. This turns out to be a moral world—Kant thought of it as a community of blessed spirits of which we ourselves are members. Thus, we again reach the conclusion of previous chapters that there is an order of reality other than that of the familiar world; it is an order which contains the values of morality such as right and good, and it is an order of which we, in respect of a certain part of ourselves—namely, our moral wills—are members. The experience which we have when we will to do our duty is not an intellectual experience, nor is it with our intellects that we recognize what is right and realize what ought to be done. Indeed, for Kant, it could not be with our intellects that we realize and recognize these things, since our intellects introduce us only to the world that they have made, Kant's world of "appearance", whereas morality belongs, as we have seen, to another order of reality which exists and is real independently of ourselves. Kant calls the faculty by means of which we know this order the "practical" as opposed to the "theoretical" reason.

The recognition of the existence of this faculty introduces us to an important philosophical doctrine. An account of this doctrine will serve to join up the strands of two previous discussions by enabling us to give a meaning to the phrase used in a previous chapter, "goods in themselves",[1] while, at the same time, taking us a further stage in the development of an objective theory of ethics by providing an additional argument against Subjectivism.

(5) The Concept of Things which are Good in Themselves

According to Kant, it is by the practical reason—a faculty closely analogous to the modern concept of intuition—that we perceive our duty and will to do it. What is more, we will it because it is right and ought to be done, irrespective of any consequences which may follow from the doing it or from the not doing it. This conclusion suggests a further argument against the subjectivist account of the development of the moral consciousness. The argument is as follows. When we are considering a moral judgment "this is right" or "this ought to be done", the subjectivist theory, as we have seen, analyzes the judgment into "this is thought right because it will be of advantage to me", or "this ought to be done because this and conduct like this tends to the survival of my community and so wins social approval." Morality, therefore, never stands on its own feet; it is always pursued for the sake of something else; it is valued as a means to an end, a non-moral end which, it is believed, will be furthered by what is called moral conduct.

Two objections are suggested by the Kantian theory of morals. Upon the first, that the analysis overlooks the uniqueness of the feeling which the notion of "right" inspires, I have already touched. It is a feeling which is manifestly different from the calculating process upon which we are accustomed to embark when we plan means to an end, as, for example, the times of the trains that we must catch, and the number of changes that we must make, in order to accomplish a cross-country railway journey. It is falsifying psychology to suggest that the feeling of moral obligation is akin to a conscious making of calculations; what is more, we

[1] See Chapter 3, p. 70.

may well feel entitled to doubt whether so unique a feeling can ever have evolved from the experience of making calculations.

Secondly, and more importantly, if Subjectivism is right, what account are we to give of the advantages for the sake of which, on the subjectivist view, morality is pursued? If morality is a means to an end, what is the end? Presumably, it is some form of good. What good? The most obvious answer is the experiencing of pleasant and the avoidance of painful sensations. Thus, let us suppose that I face danger like a courageous man, performing feats of heroism for which I am accorded the Victoria Cross. And not only the Victoria Cross, but the moral approval of my society, so that I am held up as a model at Old Boys' gatherings and am the subject of perorations at Prize-Day speeches. Now the view we are considering requires us to suppose that my courageous action is not performed by me and praised by others because courage is a virtue; because brave deeds ought to be performed for their own sake; or because it is my duty to serve and to save my comrades if I can; or because it would be disgraceful to run away. It maintains that my action and actions like mine, and the character which enables me and others like me to perform them, conduce to the survival and welfare of my social group, whether platoon, regiment, army or nation, and that it is for this reason that my platoon, regiment, army or nation encourages people to perform such actions with the tangible baits of promotion and the Victoria Cross, and the intangible ones of public esteem and a good conscience. Courage, in short, is honored because it is a means to my personal satisfaction—I should feel a skunk, if I ran away and my friends would shame me—and to the social welfare of the community to which I belong! that social welfare is desirable is taken for granted.

What account, then, are we to give of social welfare? It is, presumably, the condition of a community which consists of happy, healthy and prosperous citizens. Why are healthy citizens desirable? Presumably because health is a means to happiness. Why are prosperous citizens esteemed? Because, presumably, they are free from the fear of poverty and can satisfy their needs for food, clothing and shelter and gratify their tastes for luxury and display—can, in other words, enjoy delightful experiences and pleasant sensations. Prosperity, in short, is a means to happiness. Why, then, we must now ask, is happiness in citizens a thing to be desired? I can think of no answer to this; we must content ourselves with saying that the desirability of happiness is obvious. Our answer, then, to the question: "What ends, on the subjectivist view, are desirable?" is that happiness is such an end. Happiness, in fact, is desired as a good in itself, and other so-called goods, such as health, wealth and, we may add, power and prosperity are desired as means to happiness. Here we must once again press our question—for it has become crucial to the argument—how do I know that happiness, for the sake of which these other goods are desired, is itself a good? If the other goods are means, how do I know that happiness is the end? Suppose, for example, that somebody denies it, as some ascetics are said to have done, maintaining that we should mortify the flesh here in the interests of blessedness hereafter, or, simply because the flesh is wicked and should be mortified. What can we say in reply to such doubters?

That the Desirability of Ultimate Ends cannot be Proved or Justified

As far as I can see, there is nothing that we can say that is likely to convince them. Indeed, there is nothing we can say at all except, "We just see happiness to be a good; don't you?" And if they reply, "No, we don't," there is nothing to add. We can only observe that they lack an intuition which we possess, or that their intuitions differ from ours.

I cannot, then, in the last resort, support my intuition of the ultimate value of happiness. I can say, of course, that everybody, or almost everybody I have ever known shares this intuition of mine, but that is only a roundabout way of saying that most people feel as I do: moreover, the fact that I can claim a majority vote on my side does not prove my estimate to be correct, any more than the fact of his being in a minority will weaken the convictions of my hypothetical doubter.

This suggests an important conclusion in regard to ethics— namely, that the desirability of an ultimate good cannot be established by reason or justified at the bar of reason. An ultimate good is just seen to be desirable or, as it is sometimes put, its desirability is intuitively perceived. This conclusion in regard to ultimate goods applies to the ultimate ends of all our actions, precisely because the ultimate ends of action are ultimate goods. Take, for example, my present action in writing this book; why, it may be asked, do I write it? Three possible reasons immediately present themselves: first, that I want money; secondly, that I want fame; thirdly, that I want to increase in myself and to communicate to others, knowledge that I believe to be true. These reasons are not, of course, exhaustive and they are not mutually exclusive; my motives may be mixed—they usually are—and include all three.

The Ends of Money, Fame and Truth

Why do I want money? We have already glanced at the answer to this question. In order that I may be free from the fear of poverty, may purchase goods and may enjoy the consideration of my fellows. All these motives, as we have seen, can be analyzed into the desire to enjoy certain feelings and sensations which I have reason to believe will be pleasant.

Why fame? Some believe fame to be a good in itself. Fame is one of the objects of ambition and many have sacrificed all other goods in order to achieve it. For most of us, however, analysis exhibits fame as a means, a means to agreeable emotions. Nobody wants to be famous all by himself; in fact, the notion of solitary fame is a contradiction in terms, although some contrive to be comforted by the conviction that, ignored by their contemporaries, their merits will be recognized and their names celebrated by posterity. (One is entitled to believe anything one pleases about posterity; one of the advantages of the belief in posthumous fame is that posterity is not available to gainsay it.) Fame is also desired because of the gratification that it affords to human vanity; because it flatters self-esteem and ministers to conceit. "There", they say, "goes the famous Mr. X". The "famous Mr. X" gets asked to preside at this, to speak at that, to give away the prizes at the other; wherever he appears he is the center of interest, the cynosure of every eye, the object of the attentions of pretty women and influential men. He sits at the hostess's right hand at the head of the table of life. For him are reserved the juiciest of its meats and the most delectable of its wines. How agreeable for Mr. X! And, knowing all this— so the reasoning goes—he sits up at night to write books on philosophy in order that he may win the fame which brings him these delights.

The reasoning is plausible, though it does not, I think, cover all the ground. So far as it goes, however, it suggests that fame is desired because of the special kind of happiness that it brings to ambitious men.

What of the desire to advance in the knowledge of truth and to communicate it to others? Is this an end in itself?

Personally I think that it is, but I do not know how to establish my opinion. In all ages men have believed that the pursuit of truth, the discovery of what is the case in regard to this puzzling universe in which we live, was a legitimate object of human endeavor. The quest for truth has been the driving force which has inspired the efforts of philosophers, scientists and historians laboring often without thought of fame or hope of reward.

Nevertheless, truth is an austere goddess and few men have been content to serve her in obscurity. To discover truth is not, for most of us, enough. For truth is a mistress whom we do not wish to keep to ourselves; so soon as we believe ourselves to have found her, we wish to show her to the world. No creed or sect is without the desire to proselytize; no inventor is content to sit in his laboratory and contemplate his invention; no historian to let his history go unpublished; there is no crank or bore who will not take you into the cozy corner of his private intellectual club whence you cannot, without rudeness, escape, that he may the better impart to you in confidence his particular 'ism or 'ogy. In short, our belief in the discovery and possession of truth brings the desire to communicate what we have discovered, which is, I suppose, one of the reasons why men write books!

Things Which are Desired for their Own Sake

The foregoing conclusion means that, in so far as the *reputation* for having discovered truth is desired, it is so desired only because truth is itself held to be desirable— is, that is to say, something which is desired for its own sake. But I cannot say why it is so desired. Indeed, I do not know how to demonstrate in regard to anything that is desired for its own sake *why* it is so desired. For to show why a thing is desired, is to specify something else for the sake of which it is desired. Quinine is desired because it prevents colds; the prevention of colds, because having a cold militates against health; health because . . . I am not sure that I know why health is desired. Many would say that health is a good in itself, in which case health is desired for itself. But suppose we take the analysis further and say that health is desired because it is a means to happiness? Why, then, is happiness desired? Again I reply that I do not know; I just see it to be desirable. Or, perhaps, if we were sophisticated, we might say that health means adjustment to our environment; or that it furthers the purposes of evolution. But why should we be adjusted to our environment, and why should the purposes of evolution be furthered? Again I do not know. If we say that these things conduce to happiness we are once again setting up happiness as our ultimate good.

The conclusion of these examples may now be generalized. When we desire a thing, we either desire it for the sake of something else that it will promote or to which it will conduce; or we desire it for itself. If we desire it for the sake of something else, desire A, for example, for the sake of B, then the same position presents itself in regard to B. B is desired for the sake of C, C for that of D, and so on, until we come to something for the sake of which A B C and D are desired, something which we desire for itself and not for the sake of something else; desire, then, as an end and not merely as a means. Since any reason that we can give for supposing a thing to be desirable takes the form of specifying some other thing for the sake of which it is desired, when we come to something which is desired for itself we can give no reason why it is desired and no reason for thinking it to be desirable. We just see it to be so. The goodness of ultimate ends is, in fact, intuitively perceived, and in saying this, I am saying also that no reasons can be given why they are good. That is why I was unable, in the course of the foregoing argument, to give any satisfactory reason for the desire to discover and spread truth.

Is Happiness the only Ultimate End?

What, then, are the ends that men desire intuitively and for themselves? There has been a general consensus of opinion among philosophers that they are four—moral goodness, truth, beauty and happiness. If these four ends are desired for their own sakes, then, the states of mind which consist in their apprehension and enjoyment are "good in themselves."[1] It is customary among philosophers to denominate

[1] See Chapter 2, p. 70–71, for the first employment of this phrase.

those ends which are desired for their own sake "values". States of mind which are "good in themselves" are, therefore, those which consist in the pursuit, apprehension or enjoyment of "values". I cannot here enter into the reasons which have led philosophers to limit the number of values to four. In the last resort, as we have already seen, no reason can be given why these four ends should be valued in and for themselves—should, that is to say, be regarded as ultimate values, since any reason would take the form of specifying some more ultimate end for the sake of which they were valued, and if there were, in fact, a more ultimate end, then these four would not themselves be ultimate values, would not, therefore, be desired for their own sakes. It would be, however, for those who wish to philosophize on their own accounts, an exercise at once interesting and illuminating to take as an example anything that a man wants to do or happens to desire or wishes to become—digging in one's garden, for example, going for a walk in the country, possessing a television set, reading a new novel, or becoming chief accountant, first mate, strong-willed or immune from the temptation of drink—and to conduct an analysis, with the object of showing how each and all of these activities of doing, possessing and becoming and the conditions at which they aim resolve themselves into activities designed to promote goodness, truth, beauty, or the enjoyment of agreeable states of mind.

Hedonism

A word must be said about a well-known ethical theory— I referred to it above[1]—which maintains that there is not a number of values but that there is only one, namely, pleasure or happiness, and that whatever we desire to do, or to possess, or to become, is in the last resort desired for the sake of the happiness which we expect to derive therefrom. This view has a long history and was urged in the nineteenth century with considerable force and persuasiveness by Jeremy Bentham and John Stuart Mill, who maintained that happiness was the only source of value and the only worthy object of desire, and that the promotion of the greatest happiness of the greatest number of people should be at once the purpose of social and political action and the test of its value.

[1] See pp. 119.

This view is usually known as Ethical Hedonism, from the Greek word *hedone*, which means "pleasure", since it maintains that pleasure is the only thing which is ultimately good. A variant of this view, which is known as Psychological Hedonism, is that pleasure is the only *possible* object of human desire. The first form of the view is called ethical because it gives a standard of values and prescribes an "ought"; people "ought" it says, if they are wise, to aim only at pleasure or happiness, since pleasure is the only good. The second is psychological because it makes a statement about human psychology. It says that we are so constituted that we *can* only desire our own pleasure. A very plausible case can be made out in favor of Psychological Hedonism which is often found particularly persuasive by those who have for the first time turned their attention to the issues raised by this controversy. For a statement of this case I must refer readers to my *Guide to the Philosophy of Morals and Politics,* Chapter XI.

In my opinion, however, and in that of most philosophers, it breaks down:

(1) Because it overlooks the manifest fact that we desire some things and activities for themselves without reflecting upon whether they will or will not bring us pleasure, as, for example, food when we are hungry or the experience of going to a concert, the *motive* for going to the concert being not to get pleasure, but to hear music.

(2) Because it overlooks the purely instinctive and impulsive actions which we frequently perform, which, since they are an out-pouring of energy, a letting off of psychological steam, are not designed to secure any end; for example, singing in one's bath or breaking the furniture in a tantrum.

(3) Because it puts the cart before the horse by falsely suggesting that, because we have found certain things and activities to be followed by agreeable sensations, we therefore desire the agreeable sensations that follow them, whereas, in point of fact, unless we first desired the things and activities for themselves—unless, that is to say, they were intrinsically desirable—they would not bring agreeable sensations. Let me put this diagramatically. Because pleasure P occurs when I obtain something X which, I want, therefore, the hedonist maintains, I only want X

because of P. But if I had not wanted X for its own sake, I should not have experienced P on obtaining it; P, in short, only occurs because I wanted X independently of P; hence, that we should desire things other than pleasure is a necessary condition of our experiencing pleasure when we obtain them.

(4) Because it gives an inadequate explanation of self-sacrifice and unselfishness, of the martyr who goes to his death at the stake, or of the hungry mother who gives her own share of the food to her children.

If, however, it be maintained not that pleasure is the only possible object of desire (Psychological Hedonism), but that pleasure is the only thing that is ultimately good (Ethical Hedonism), and the only thing, therefore, that *ought* to be desired, we must ask how the fact that it is, if it is a fact, is known? How is the hedonist to defend the proposition to somebody who presumes to doubt it? I do not know. He can only say to him, as I said above, "I see happiness to be desirable; in fact I see it to be the only thing that, in the long run, is desirable. Don't you?" And if the doubter replies that he does not, the hedonist has no more to say. Again we reach the conclusion which we have already noted, that happiness, being an ultimate good, shares with whatever other ends are ultimate the characteristic of being perceived to be good *as an end* by a process of direct intuition; it is not established as an ultimate good by a process of ratiocination. This being so, its desirability cannot be either demonstrated or defended by reason. But if he admits this, as in the last resort he must, in regard to the value of happiness, what reply is the hedonist who invokes happiness as the only ultimate end, the only thing which is, therefore, desirable for its own sake, to make to the man who maintains that other things are desirable for their own sake as well; that, in fact, there is not one value but several?

Admittedly the upholder of the existence of several values cannot demonstrate that truth, goodness and beauty are goods in themselves, if their ultimate value is questioned; but neither can the advocate of the exclusive valuableness of happiness or pleasure. We are here in a region where neither proof nor disproof is possible; all that we can do is to call in witness the general experience of mankind, which, as I have pointed out, is impressively in favor of the view that the other three values are also desired as ultimate ends, and ask the hedonist whether, having looked as closely as he can into his own consciousness, he can put his hand on his heart and honestly affirm that, when he ascends a hill to look at a sunset, he does so because he tells himself that the sight of the sunset will make him happy; or that when he takes off his boots and paddles across a stream, he does so because he thinks that the process of paddling will make him happy and not because he wants to get to the other side; or that when he takes up this book and wades through its occasionally wearisome pages, he does so because he thinks it will make him happy, and not because he wishes to learn something about philosophy.

The Argument Returns to Subjectivism

This conclusion has a further application which brings us back to our objections against subjectivist theories of ethics, and enables us to bring home to roost a further objection to Subjectivism. Confronted with an apparently ethical judgment the subjectivist reveals the non-ethical origins, from which, he holds, it is derived, or points to the non-ethical considerations which originally led to its being passed. For "This ought to be done because it is right" he substitutes "I have a feeling of obligation which impels me to do this and I shall have a feeling of guilt if I don't do it, because this, and conduct like this, wins and has always won the approval of my community." Why does it win approval? "Because in the long run it conduces to the survival and welfare of the community."

At this point we propose to put the question, what is meant by survival and welfare? We have seen[1] that these expressions are, at least in part, analyzable into the enjoyment of agreeable sensations. Why, then, should we desire to enjoy pleasant and agreeable sensations? "Because," says the subjectivist, "pleasure is a good." But how, we ask, do you know that pleasure is a good? To this question, as we have seen, there is no reasoned answer; the subjectivist just sees it to be so and,

[1] See above, pp. 118, 128, 129.

if pressed in this imaginary dialogue, he must in the last resort *say*, "I just see it to be so." The subjectivist's position rests, then, in the long run on the unanalyzable and indefinable intuition that pleasure is a good. I do not propose to quarrel with him for that, for, if I am right in asserting the indefensible character of ultimate goods, he can say no other. But what we can and must do is to ask him with what logic in the circumstances he presumes to dismiss the intuition which insists not that "this is pleasant and ought to be pursued", but "this is right and ought to be done".

If the ultimate value of happiness turns out in the last resort to be just assumed, with what right does the subjectivist cavil at the ultimate value of duty? And with what right, finally, does he suggest that the reduction of ethical sentiments to non-ethical ones is a rational and legitimate process, while at the same time stigmatizing the intuitionist's insistence that "I ought to do this because it is my duty", with the implied admission that that is all there is to say about it, as illegitimate and irrational? The two positions here asserted are, indeed, in the last resort on all fours. This being so, there seems to be no longer any motive for refusing to accept at their face value the intuitive deliverances of our moral consciousness, or for analyzing the unique feeling which we have for "ought" into some other kind of feeling which is not unique, as for example, our desire for pleasure or our calculations of expediency.

Conclusions

Latent Inconsistency of Naturalistic Ethics

Writers on subjectivist ethics lay claim to a hard-headed rationalism, which is impatient of mystical moonshine and moral hocus-pocus. They pride themselves on their success in explaining the facts of moral experience in terms of the concepts applicable to phenomena occurring in the natural world. Man, like the earwig and the worm, is for them a product of nature and exhibits the characteristics appropriate to his species. Among these is the instinct to survive as an individual, the instinct to co-operate with other individuals who belong to his society, and the desire for pleasure. In these terms and along these lines the subjectivist seeks to explain, and believes that with the expenditure of a little ingenuity he can succeed in explaining, the facts of moral experience. In point of fact, however, as we have seen, in basing his argument, as he cannot help but do, on the apparently unanalyzable value of happiness, whose status as a good he intuitively recognizes and irrationally accepts, the subjectivist makes his sacrifice on the altar of value no less than the objectivist, albeit he does it privily and without being aware that a sacrifice is being performed. But since a sacrifice is, in fact, performed, it may well be asked what is the point of taking so long a journey and expending such a wealth of ingenuity in the process, only at the end to find intruding itself through the back door one of those values which had so ceremoniously been kicked down the front doorsteps? Why not admit them openly from the first?

Ethics as the Revelation of Values

To do so entails the corollaries:

(1) That there is something unique about man's moral consciousness.

(2) That to say "this is right and ought to be done" is, therefore, to give expression to a unique experience and to report a unique fact about the universe.

(3) That "this is good", or "this is right", can never be satisfactorily analyzed without remainder into "this is pleasant to me", or "this wins my approval", or "the approval of my society".

(4) That ethical attributes do belong objectively and in their own right to the characters of human beings, to the courses of conduct upon which they embark, to social institutions and to codes of law.

(5) That the universe contains, therefore, a moral order in the sense that "good" and "right" are independent and objective factors in it and features of it, whether recognized by our minds or not.

(6) That the characters, actions, institutions, codes and so on which are met with in the familiar world and rec-

ognized as good or right, are recognized to be so—provided, of course, that they be rightly recognized—in virtue of their possession of a moral quality which derives from an order of reality other than that of the familiar world. By reason of their possession of that quality they are themselves, in part, members of that order.

Thus, by another route we have reached the conclusion of the two preceding chapters. The familiar world of common sense is not the only world; it may be that in the last resort it is not the real world. There is another order of reality which is immaterial and which contains values of which goodness is one. These values enter into relation with and are immanent in the everyday world, the value of goodness being immanent in human personalities.

The Transition to Theism

There is one further corollary which we have not, as yet, permitted ourselves to draw and cannot here pursue. The values, as they have so far been discussed, have been represented as ultimate but isolated factors in the universe. I have not hitherto dealt with the possibility that there may be a connection or unity between them. The real world, then, may, so far as the implications of the ethical argument are concerned, be a plurality, a plurality of values. The further question which remains to be asked is whether the values themselves form part of a whole or a unity which underlies them.

Let us, first, consider the relation of values to minds. Though it is plausible to suppose in regard to beauty and truth that they exist in complete independence of mind— there seems to be no reason why a picture or a sunset should not be lovely even if no minds regard its loveliness, or why the proposition that $(a^2 - b^2) = (a + b)(a - b)$ should not be true, even if there is no mind to know it—it is difficult to make a similar supposition in regard to happiness and goodness. Can there, one wonders, be happiness without minds or persons to be happy? It seems highly unlikely. Can there be moral goodness, which is not the goodness of persons, or which does not characterize the conduct in which they express their goodness? One is tempted to answer that there cannot. For what would such a supposition involve? First, since we are assuming values to be objective, that the universe contains a moral law or order which is as real and objective as the laws and order of physical nature; secondly, that this moral law or order is in some sense part of the ultimate reality of the universe and not—always assuming that we have rejected Subjectivism—a description of the way in which human minds happen to think, feel and judge; thirdly, that the universe happens at a certain point in its evolution to have delivered itself of minds, namely our minds, which are capable of divining and obeying this moral law, which is, nevertheless, independent of the minds which obey and divine it. But though it is independent of *our* minds can we conceive a moral law or a moral ideal which exists outside *any* mind? I doubt it, just as I doubt whether we can conceive of a happiness which is not the happiness of any person. Hence, the admission of the objective values of morality and happiness seems to imply the existence of a mind other than our own which knows and enjoys these values. If we do not accept this implication, we are faced with the following dilemma:

(1) If the moral law or ideal is known by, but is not created by and is not, therefore, dependent upon our minds, then, assuming all human minds to have gone out of existence, it is difficult to see in what medium the value of morality would manifest itself, or to what actions or characters it would attach itself.

(2) If, in order to avoid this difficulty, we make the moral law dependent for its existence upon the minds that know it, maintaining that it is wholly and exclusively manifested in our minds and characters, manifested as beauty is manifested in works of art and truth in propositions, so that without our minds as its medium of manifestation it would no longer exist, we fall into the Subjectivism which we have been engaged in criticizing, since, if this were indeed the case, morality would have no validity apart from us.

The obvious way out of this difficulty is to postulate the

existence of a mind other than our own by which morality is known, and not only known but created—to postulate, in other words, a law-giver who lays down the moral law or order of the universe. If this law-giver is also the Creator of the universe, then the moral law, since it prevails throughout the universe, will exist and be valid independent of us. Granted this assumption, we could reconcile the requirements of both sides of our dilemma, since it would be possible to maintain that the minds and characters of human beings were the medium in which the value of morality was manifested, without at the same time making morality dependent upon the minds in which it was manifested and so reducing it to a subjective status. Morality, on this view, would be dependent upon mind, but not necessarily upon *our minds,* and the universe would be a moral universe, even if there were no human minds to manifest the value of morality.

At this point the argument passes over from ethics to religion, where we cannot further follow it. I have taken it thus far in order that, having reached the point of transition, I might be in a position to add that most though by no means all writers on ethics have believed that sooner or later the bridge must be crossed; that ethics, in fact, passes over into theology precisely because if we take the fact of morality seriously, it is found to imply the existence of God.

I conclude with three observations which, without taking us beyond the point which we have reached, may serve to round off our journey.

That Morality Points to without Necessitating God

First, it is probable that the moral values which we designate by such words as goodness, right and duty, are not only known by human minds, but manifest themselves in and through human minds; that just as there could be no beauty in this world without matter, wood or stone or sound or paint or steel or film or trees or flowers or skies; just as there could be no truth without the propositions of history and science and logic and mathematics, so there could be no manifestation of moral goodness in this world without human minds and wills and emotions to serve as its medium. If there is no universal mind to prescribe a moral law and to serve as its repository independently of human minds, wills and emotions, this assertion would be tantamount to Subjectivism; if there is, it is not.

Secondly, if this world originated in a creative mind which prescribes the moral order, the knowledge of moral values by human minds is neither unreasonable nor unlikely, but if the world is mindless and haphazard, then the generation at a certain point in time of human minds with the power of knowing moral values which are just waiting to be known is, to say the least of it, very odd.

Thirdly, if there is a mind, or even a personality, at the heart of the universe, the values may well be the medium through which its nature is manifested, the modes under which it permits itself to be known by us. On this supposition, just as happiness and goodness are manifested in particular human minds, truth in particular propositions, beauty in particular physical things, so God's nature is manifested in the universal values, happiness, goodness, truth and beauty. On this view, the physical world of familiar things is, as Plato would say, two removes from reality. First, it is the medium in which the real world of universal values is manifested; secondly, the universal values are themselves the medium in which God is manifested.

On this view, moreover, the universe, as the monists have maintained,[1] is a single whole or unity; this unity is God, who expresses Himself in the different values just as they express themselves in the infinite variety of finite phenomena.

Note.—I ought in fairness to my readers to point out that these last observations represent speculations of my own rather than the conclusions of the thoughts of others. It is one of the results of contact with great minds that our own lesser minds should by them be stimulated to activity along the lines of thought that they have traced. When the pioneers have blazed a trail, it is easier for the generations that follow to branch off from the main track along little paths of their own making. I mention the point both by way of encouragement and of warning; by way of encouragement, because it may help the reader to realize, by illustrative example, that philosophy is not all taking in and never giving out, but is also an

[1] See Chapter 4, pp. 95, 96.

independent activity of exploration by the minds of those who, having taken in copiously and often, may sometimes be moved to give a little out; by way of warning, because it is important for the reader to realize that the later speculations of this chapter own no better authority than the initiative of their author.

Chapter 6

THE PHILOSOPHY OF POLITICS

Plan of Chapter

IN the last chapter I tried to show how an examination of the facts of the moral consciousness leads to a revelation of values, and that theories of ethics, which seek to eliminate or to whittle away the objectivity of moral values, fail to do justice to these facts. I propose in this chapter to undertake a similar inquiry in regard to politics. The purpose of ethics, according to the Greek philosophers, was to prescribe the nature of the good life for the individual; of politics, the nature of the good life for communities of individuals. But ethics and politics, they taught, interlock: (*a*) because the good life for communities of individuals—that is to say, for States—is desirable only in so far as it is a condition of and a means to the living of good lives by individual citizens. In this sense, politics is ancillary to ethics.

(*b*) Because the good life for man is the good life of man the citizen; it can, in other words, be lived only in co-operation with his fellows in society. In this sense politics is part of ethics, and the ethical life cannot be prescribed or pursued without taking into account man's relation to society.

(*c*) Because it is the business of the wise legislator to lay down general rules for the living of the good life by members of the community, and so to develop the minds of the citizens by education and to mould their characters by training that they may be able to live it and desirous of living it. In this sense the art of the statesman is, Aristotle taught, the supreme art, since it prescribes the nature of well-being for the community as a whole. It is entailed by this conception that it is the business of the statesman to determine what the nature of the good life for the individual is. I shall comment upon this view later in the chapter.[1] Such, briefly, were the conclusions of Aristotle in regard to the relation between ethics and politics.

[1] See pp. 169–170, below.

Following his lead, I shall endeavor in this chapter to treat political philosophy with a view to the revelation of the objective ends or values which underlie the purposes of political action.

I shall inquire first, what ends do, in fact, guide the policies of States, and consider in what respects they are satisfactory and in what respects unsatisfactory. Secondly, I shall examine the ends which politicians *profess* to be the objectives of their policies and seek to show that these are usually different from the aims which, in fact, inspire them; it is the professed rather than the achieved aims of political action which, when analyzed, reveal the presence of underlying values. Finally, I shall consider what the social values are, and seek to exhibit them as concerned with the establishment of those conditions in which the objective values of ethics —happiness, goodness, beauty and truth—may be pursued by individual citizens. If this endeavor is successful, it will have had the effect of exhibiting politics as the means to the achievement of the objective values of ethics.

1. The Ends which Communities do, in fact, Pursue. That they are Unsatisfactory

What are the ends which States pursue and which, therefore, politicians and civil servants, who direct and carry out the policies of States, value? They are many, but, for the purposes of illustration, three will serve. They are power, prestige and wealth.

(a) Power as an End

That States desire power is undeniable. The possession of an empire is everywhere acclaimed as a good; loss of territory as an evil. Large populations tend to make States powerful and, therefore, loss of population is also accounted an evil. When States, through the mouths of politicians, speak of "their sacred mission", their "national interest", or their "historic destiny", what they mean is that they have a "mission" to acquire territory—that is, to increase their power— that their "interests" demand an extension of power and that their "destiny", whether conceived as God, or fate, or the movement of history, or the compulsion of their own "genius", has marked them out for such an extension.

What, then, is power? Power is the ability to impose your will upon other human beings, by inflicting injury upon them, if they refuse to submit to it. Power has, of course, many forms: there is the power of money, the power of place, the power of birth and blood and the power of learning; above all, there is the power of superior force. All these forms of power have this in common, that if men withstand or affront the power-holder, then he can cause them to undergo disagreeable experiences by putting them out of business (money power), refusing to promote them at the office (power of place), refusing to invite them and their wives to parties and dinners (power of birth and blood), or by quite simply fining or confining or hurting them (power of superior force). When States committed to a policy of expansion, embarked on a career of conquest or hot in pursuit of Empire, demand that the territory under their rule be extended, what they, in fact, desire is to be in a position to impose their wills upon undeveloped peoples, subject territories, inferior economic classes, or differently pigmented races. Now, this exercise of the State's will is accepted either willingly or unwillingly. If it is accepted unwillingly, then the imposition of one's will by force upon those who wish to be free to act in accordance with their own wills, is not ethically admirable; the point has only to be put and it is immediately clear that it is not. If it is accepted willingly, then there is no need for power to enforce it.

It is sometimes said that power may be justifiably exercised by communities against other communities because these óther communities are wicked and ought to be punished; or because they are undeveloped and ought to be protected, or civilized. Thus, the Nazis exercised power against the Jews because they were wicked; Catholics against Protestants because they were heretical; while the British took over undeveloped territories for the benefit of natives who were benighted.

But, (i) the belief in the peculiar wickedness of whole peoples cannot be sustained; even if it could, it is not the duty of other peoples to punish them for being what they are.

(ii) The view that undeveloped peoples are improved by being "developed" is open to question. The South Sea islanders, for example, were probably happier, and were certainly more dignified, before Western civilization gave them missionaries, bibles, gin, syphilis, cheap cotton goods, radios and canned foods.

(iii) No community is entitled to feel so certain of the superiority of its own way of life as to be justified in imposing it by force on another people.

Physical benefits, such as roads, bridges, sanitation, irrigation, transport, medical science can, no doubt, justifiably be conferred by more civilized upon less civilized peoples, but history shows that there are few if any cases in which these benefits have been given disinterestedly—given, that is to say, where there was no prospect of acquisition of territory, no hope of acquiring raw materials, or no intention of enlisting supplies of cheap labor.

(iv) The alleged beneficial effects to people B of being ruled over by people A are always stressed by the statesmen of people A; they are never, so far as I am aware, demanded by the statesmen of people B. Empires and Colonies, in other words, are acquired on the initiative of the rulers and colonizers not at the instance of the ruled and the colonized. This being so, the alleged benefits to people B of the rule of people A look uncommonly like rationalizations[1] by people A of their real motives for acquiring power over people B.

(v) The implied conclusion that desire for power leads to self-deception with regard to motives is the least of the evil effects of power upon the power-pursuer. Of all appetites, the appetite for power grows the most quickly and the most surely with what it feeds on. Power corrupts character and obscures judgment; it makes kind men cruel, good-natured men grasping and fallible men self-righteous. The philosopher's verdict on the effects of power can be read in the account of the "tyrannical man" in the Ninth Book of Plato's *Republic;* the historian's, in Lord Acton's terrible verdict upon the record of human history, "all power corrupts and absolute power corrupts absolutely." I conclude that power is not a good in itself, whether it is pursued by States or by individuals. Whether power is good or not depends upon how it is used and upon its effects upon those who use it and are subject to its use. Power, in fact, when it is good, is good as a means to something else.

(b) Prestige as an End

Prestige is bound up with military greatness, indeed according to many statesmen, it is determined by it. Thus, ac-

---

[1] See Chapter 5, p. 112, for the technical sense in which this word is used.

cording to Mussolini, a typical exponent of power politics, "the prestige of nations is determined almost absolutely by their military glories and their armed power." Military greatness is, perhaps, the commonest of all the standards which are invoked by historians and politicians when estimating the worth of States. Yet military greatness depends upon the possession of efficiency in the arts of slaughter; it is because of their known efficiency in this respect, that States are in a position to impose their will upon other States. This, to put it bluntly, is neither more nor less than the power of the bully to impose his will upon others unless they submit; it is, in a word, the power of blackmail. Not a very winsome attribute, one would have thought, nor one pre-eminently in consonance with the tenets of the principles of Christ, in which Western civilization professes to believe. One of the many drawbacks of military power is that, sooner or later, the State which possesses it is driven by force of circumstances or by its own ambition to put it to the test—in other words, States which possess military power are given to aggression. Yet history shows that aggressive militarism has always ruined, sooner or later, the nation that practices it. Unable to control their incurably mischievous aggressiveness, the Greek States decimated themselves and their neighbors in wars, until through failure to unite before a common foe they fell under the dominion of Macedon. The most militarily successful phases of Carthaginian history preceded the utter destruction of Carthage, and Hannibal, the greatest military genius that Carthage produced, was the architect of that destruction. All through history, militarily successful and energetically aggressive peoples, especially if led by men of genius, have under-estimated their enemies, have deluded themselves with myths of short, decisive wars ending in victory, have failed to make due allowance for the factor of time, have, indeed, gone from blunder to blunder with such persistence and unanimity that, if history is read realistically, the production of a military genius is one of the greatest disasters that can happen to a people.

Napoleon, for example, was a disaster to France. He reduced the number of Frenchmen, diminished their stature, and loaded them with debts. He brought loneliness and misery to many women and gross physical agony to many men. Why, then, should the ability to produce a Napoleon or any

number of Napoleons be accounted a merit in a State? The
answer is not clear.

I conclude that military prestige is not a good in itself.
One must consider how it is acquired and upon what it
rests. One must also ask what causes it supports, what movements it assists, and what purposes it serves. One must ask,
in fact, how it is used. Prestige, then, like power, when it is
good, is good as a means.

(c) Wealth as an End

There are some who desire the appearance of possessing
wealth as much or almost as much as its possession, but the
appearance would not be thought desirable, unless the reality
was desired; hence, we need concern ourselves only with the
possession of wealth considered as an end. Is wealth, then, a
good in itself? Wealth is accounted a good in itself only by
misers; most of us want money for what it will buy; we also
want it because of the estimation in which its supposed
possession causes us to be held by others. If we use it to
spread happiness and enlightenment, to assist the poor, to
succor the needy, to help the distressed, to raise the general
level of taste; if, moreover, we do all this without patronage,
expecting no return and exacting no service, our wealth may
be said to be well used. If, however, we use it to acquire
possessions because, like Americans and business men, we
measure the value of men in terms of their incomes, and we
are, therefore, anxious to acquire as many proofs of income
as possible, our wealth is employed to minister to pride and
support self-complacency.

Men also value wealth because money gives them power
over others; but there is no *merit* in acquiring or possessing
the power of money. Broadly speaking, money is acquired in
one of two ways; it is left to us or made by us. To be left
money is a sign of luck rather than of virtue, since in most
cases the receipt of an inheritance is determined by the bedroom in which a man happens to have been born, an event
over which, presumably, he had no control. To have made
money means either that you have been successful in over-
reaching your competitors—but astuteness, far-sightedness,
predatoriness, though virtues in the gambler or the poker
player, are not morally desirable qualities in the citizen—or
that you have the luck to possess some special faculty or

attribute, a melodious voice, a lovely face, a droll wit, a quick eye or a nimble foot at games—but such possessions though of great value to their possessors are not moral virtue—or that, desiring money more than anything else, you have sacrificed everything else to its accumulation. To sacrifice everything to a single aim indicates strength of will and a restricted outlook, but it is not in itself morally meritorious. I conclude that the possessing of money and the power of money, whether the money is left to you or made by you, is not in itself a good; in so far as money is good, it is good as a means and not as an end.

The Defects of Communities which Value Wealth

This becomes clearer when we turn from the possessing of wealth by individuals, to the possessing of wealth by communities. For immediately we find ourselves faced by one of the many anomalies of modern society—namely, the unequal distribution of wealth among citizens. Before the war Great Britain was commonly and rightly accounted one of the wealthiest States in the world, yet her wealth was distributed very unevenly, with the result that, according to a report published by Sir John Orr in 1938, 22,500,000 of the inhabitants of England and Wales were living on a diet below the minimum standard of health, while 4½ million were living on a weekly income of 10s. per head, of which only 4s. was spent on food.

I am not writing a book on politics, so I leave the political moral to be drawn by others; my concern is with philosophy and, more particularly, with the philosophy of values, in whose pursuit, as I tried to show in the previous chapter, the true end of life is to be found. From this standpoint the existing system of wealth distribution has two defects:

(1) First at the top of the scale, the rich, as we have seen, tend to value money-power as an end. Therefore, they devote the major part of their energies to the acquisition of money. It follows:

(a) That they have a false scale of values, as a result of which they under-estimate, or are ignorant of, true goods such as beauty and knowledge.

(b) They have neither the time nor the energy to pursue true values, and, in the course of a lifetime devoted to the pursuit of false values, lose both the capacity and the will to pursue true ones. For human nature is moulded to the stuff in which it works, and a settled habit of valuing money and power as ends blunts our apprehension of beauty, and makes us incurious in regard to knowledge and insensitive to the finer points of human relationship. These results emerge most clearly from a consideration of the use which is made by the rich of their leisure. Take, for example, the case of the retired business man. All his life he had been engaged in making money in order that one day he may retire and enjoy his gains. The age of retirement comes, and for a time, bereft of his accustomed hard labor, he endeavors to make his existence tolerable with the aid of sport, games, cocktails, dancing, speeding, the theater, and a little unconvincing love-making on the Riviera. Sated by these amusements, he is driven to take to big-game hunting, desert exploring, mountain climbing, or some other dangerous and disagreeable pursuit on which he can persuade other people to accompany him only by offering them large salaries, and finally retires disgustedly to his desk, in despair of finding life tolerable without the hard labor to which he has been accustomed.

(2) Secondly, at the bottom of the scale, most human beings are rendered incapable of living the good life by four considerations:

(*a*) They work too long and exhaust their energies, blunt their sensibilities and expend their spirits in getting the means to make life possible.

(*b*) They work at dull and drudging tasks which do not fire their imaginations, exercise their reasons, or call out the full stretch of their faculties. They are, therefore, literally undeveloped men and women. Moreover, their work consists very largely in the management and tendance of machines, the effect of continual intercourse with which is to close the avenues of the mind, to restrict its activities and to reduce its interests to those of schoolboys and mechanics. "How does it work, daddy?" is an appropriate question when it is asked by my son aged 12, but it is inappropriate in a full-grown man who should be concerned not with the mode of its working, but with the purposes *for* which it works.

(c) They are inadequately educated, so that they are unable to realize their potentialities and get the most out of life by bringing to it the most that is in themselves. Their faculty for the appreciation of great work in art and literature remains, for example, undeveloped.

(d) Their ends are restricted by the circumstances of their lot. Enough to eat and drink, a comfortable house to live in, a secure job, provision for sickness and unemployment, with an occasional visit to the seashore or the movies—these, for most of them, exhaust the conception of "goods".

Most human beings who have ever lived have not even enjoyed these limited goods. Is it any wonder that those who find themselves suddenly endowed with them value them beyond reason, and equate them with the whole "good for man"?

It is interesting in this connection to observe that the mechanical arts and crafts, including applied science and such work as is now done by technicians and engineers, were denounced by the two great philosophers of antiquity, Plato and Aristotle, because they left a man no leisure to make the best of his body and his mind. The continual practice of them stamps both body and mind with the soullessness, regularity and uniformity of the mechanical medium to which body and mind are subdued.

The conclusion is that the valuing by communities of wealth as an end issues in the production of citizens who are ignorant of the true ends of life and do not know how their lives should be lived. Of the art of living they know little or nothing; they are too preoccupied with the acquisition of the means to make life possible, thus sacrificing the end to the means.

I have taken three examples of the objects which communities do, in fact, value—power, prestige and wealth—and shown that they are not entitled to be regarded in themselves as the rightful ends of human endeavor. When they are good, they are good as means to ends which lie beyond them.

2. The Ends which Communities profess to Pursue.
That they are, in fact, Means

These are numerous and various. A good general statement

of them is afforded by the four freedoms of the Atlantic Charter—freedom from fear, freedom from want, freedom of expression and freedom of worship. I am not, I venture to repeat, writing a treatise on politics; my concern is to analyze political conceptions, in order to see what light they throw on the nature of value. I am, then, under no obligation to make an exhaustive list of the ends professed by statesmen. Three will be sufficient for the illustration of my theme. The three which I have selected are Social Justice, Liberty and Education.

Social Justice

Social Justice includes freedom from want; it also includes a fairer distribution of the community's wealth than at present obtains, and the extending to every citizen of the right to make the most of himself and his talents in the interest both of his own development and of that of the community to which he belongs. Two different ideals are involved here which require separate treatment. Freedom from want is a comprehensive phrase covering all that we mean by "economic goods", a fair wage, a secure job, provision for oneself and for one's family when one falls sick or falls out of a job, a good and comfortable house with "a bit of garden", adequate leisure, lighted and paved streets, a sanitary system, a hospital system and so on. Do these things constitute "goods in themselves"? I think that they do not. They only seem to be goods to those who are deprived of them, or who enjoy them in too small measure, or who must fight to get them, or who hold them insecurely, just as health, which is taken for granted by the healthy man, is accounted a good by the asthmatic who must fight to draw each difficult and painful breath into his straining lungs. That this is so, may be seen by a consideration of the behavior of those to whom these things come easily and as of right. The kings, the emperors, the caliphs, the sultans, the aristocrats, the business men, even the secure and the established middle classes, do not take these things for goods; they take them for granted. That there should be an adequate supply of money, that there should be security, that there should be a roof over one's head and a fire in one's room, that there should be indoor sanitation, that there should be tables spread with food four times a day—these things seemed to the upper and middle classes of prosperous Victorian England part of the natural order of the universe. They no more accounted them goods than they accounted the air that they breathed. Nor, indeed, would any human beings to whom they came naturally, easily, securely and as of right, regard them as goods. For these things are valued, in so far as they are valued at all, as a means to other things; if they are absent, then these other things are put out of reach. If a man is thinking continuously about his job, he cannot think about poetry; if he is cold or hungry, he cannot enjoy music; if he is apprehensive or afraid, he cannot give his mind to science or philosophy; if he must regard his friends as potential competitors for a few precarious jobs, then he cannot disinterestedly enjoy and value their friendship. I conclude that the goods included under the term Social Justice, of which "freedom from want" may serve as a typical example, are valuable as a background to and condition of the good life, not as part of it. In their absence we cannot enjoy the good life nor, if our minds are wholly preoccupied with them, can we pursue those ends which are good in themselves; but, once they are present and securely present, we become habituated to them and take them for granted, with the result that they sink into the background of our consciousness.

The other ideal covered by the term Social Justice is equality. When men demand equality, the demand does not, of course, mean that they think that all men are equal, though it has often been falsely charged against the advocates of equality that the natural equality of all men was what they maintained. It must be admitted that the language used by the advocates of equality has lent countenance to this misinterpretation; for example, that of the American Declaration of Independence, which misleadingly asserts in its second paragraph, "All men are created free and equal." What is it, then, that the doctrine of equality intends to assert? I suggest the following three propositions:

(1) All men are equally important in the sight of God, precisely because they are His creatures and His children.

(2) All men are equally important to themselves.

(3) Effect can only be given by the State to propositions (1) and (2), if it extends to all its citizens an equal opportunity of developing themselves and showing what

they have it in them to be. In other words, it must treat them as if they were all equally important to it.

Equality, then, is not a good in itself. It is a means, and a necessary means, to something else—namely, the opportunity for the self-development and realization of citizens and of all the citizens.

Liberty and Education

These need not detain us long; they lead to the same conclusion as our examination of Social Justice, and a short treatment should be sufficient to reveal it. Liberty of speech, liberty of action, liberty to read and to write, are not felt to be goods, except by those to whom they are denied. The generation in which I grew up took them for granted, as witness the following extract from Professor Bury's book *History of Freedom of Thought,* which appeared in 1913. "The struggle of reason against authority has ended in what appears now to be a decisive and permanent victory for liberty. In the most civilized and progressive countries freedom of discussion is recognized as a fundamental principle." And because we did take them for granted, we did not realize how hardly they had been won and how precariously they were maintained; Fascism has disillusioned us, and all Europe craves today[1] for the freedom which tyrants have denied. Nevertheless, freedom is not a positive, but a negative good. It is like health or air. We normally value health only when we have lost it or, having lost it, have just regained it, while the memory of illness is still vividly with us. Similarly with air; we value it only if it is taken from us, when we value it so much that we proceed to die unless it is restored to us. So men normally value liberty only when it is denied to them, but its denial is a denial of all that makes life worth living, so that the spirit of the prisoner cries out for liberty and again for liberty, as the lungs of the man who is choking cry out for air; liberty, indeed, is the air of the spirit. Air and health are means to an efficient and freely acting body. But we may use our efficient and freely acting bodies to beat our wives, bash the heads of our fellows, or rescue children from burning houses or sinking boats; the more efficient the body, the more efficient the beating, the bashing and the rescuing. . . .

[1] I am writing early in 1943.

Similarly, liberty is a means to an efficient and freely acting mind; but, again we must ask, will the efficient and freely acting mind be used to plan revenge, to pursue a ruthless ambition, to devise tortures or to discover the theory of relativity, organize the feeding of starving Europe, or compose Beethoven's Fifth Symphony? In other words—and the point should surely by now be clear—liberty is liberty to think something, to plan something, to devise something, to organize something, to acquire something, or to pursue something, and upon the quality of these "somethings" depends the value of the liberty with which we think, plan, devise, organize, acquire or pursue. What matters about liberty, in fact, is how we use it.

Similarly with education. An educated mind is admittedly more effective than an uneducated one; but effective for what ends? Educated men have done as much harm in the world as uneducated; in fact, they have done more. They have also done more good. If the object of education is to enable a man to realize his latent potentialities, to help him to release his energies, then upon the nature of those potentialities and of the purposes for which the energies are used will depend the value of the education. Education, in other words, is a means to good. It is not in itself a good.

The Purpose of Political Action

The point of all these illustrations is the same. Social security, social justice and the goods which they include— health, housing, employment, provision against sickness and accident—are not any more than are the political value, liberty and the social value, education, goods in themselves; they are good as means to something else, that "something else" being the effects which they confer upon the individuals who enjoy them. More precisely, they may be regarded as goods which are means to a certain kind of freedom; all of them, that is to say, set the individual free: social security from want, fear and the restraining cares of poverty; social justice from the darkening resentments of inequality and arbitrary privilege; liberty from oppressive interference with his person, leisure, time and possessions; education from the sense of social inferiority, of unused talents and restricted development.

But freedom, as we have seen, is itself a negative concept;

it is a condition of good rather than a good, since it leads inevitably to the question, how is the freedom used?

Two conclusions emerge. First, the object of political legislation is to produce certain effects upon individuals. Secondly, these effects may be most appropriately summed up under the concept of freedom from restrictions and hindrances.

Our next question is freedom from restrictions and hindrances to do or to achieve or to become what? The two answers commonly given are, first, to achieve happiness; secondly, to realize and develop one's personality. All the aspects of one's personality? Obviously not. Nobody would say that the object of political legislation was to set the individual free to develop the baser elements of his personality, so that he might become more unrestrictedly lustful, cruel and predatory than he would have been without such legislation. Clearly, then, it is only certain aspects of his personality for whose development political action should seek to provide—those, namely, which are the highest and best. We reach, then, the conclusion that the object of political action is to provide those conditions in which the individual is free to achieve happiness and to develop the highest and best aspects of and elements in his personality. Why should the State assume an obligation to further such development? The answer that has frequently been given in the history of political philosophy is that the individual has a "right" to happiness and a "right" to personal development. In order that the significance of this claim may be fully grasped, I must briefly indicate the background of the doctrine of "natural rights", as they are sometimes called, upon which it is based.

The Social Contract Theory and the Doctrine of Natural Rights

This doctrine has been historically associated with a certain theory of the origin and purpose of society. Why, political philosophers have asked, is there society at all? In answer to this question a number of philosophers in the seventeenth and eighteenth centuries propounded a theory known as the Social Contract Theory of the origin of society, according to which human beings lived originally under conditions of anarchic individualism, in which every man's hand was against his fellows and everyman's hand was against him. Finding the resultant insecurity and misery intolerable, men came together to form society in order to put an end to them. Every man, then, on this view has a right to security, protection and justice, because it was precisely for these purposes that society was formed and that men agreed to live in it.

Few philosophers now hold this view. One of the objections to it is that it assumes the validity of the argument from origins [1] in seeking to explain and interpret the present nature and purpose of society by reference to and in terms of the origins from which it is supposed to have taken its rise.

Another objection is that it is extremely doubtful whether there ever was a pre-social condition of mankind. If we begin, as Plato and Aristotle did, by defining man as a social and political animal,[2] then it follows that we must suppose him to have always lived in some kind of society however rudimentary.

If further, adopting the conclusions of the argument in regard to the meaning of the phrase "the nature of a thing" in Chapter 5,[3] we insist that the full meaning of a thing's "nature" is to be found not in the germ from which it arose, but in the highest development of which it is capable, then we shall say that it is only in society that a man can realize the full potentialities of his nature; we shall add that a man has a "right" to such development and that, since it is only in society that he can achieve it, it is the business of society to establish the conditions in which such full development is possible. The justification of "rights" is, then, to be found in the ends or purposes for which society exists rather than in the origins from which society may be supposed to have taken its rise. It follows that the end of social and political action is to be found in its effect in enabling citizens to realize their natures in the development of the highest aspects of their personalities. To put this conclusion in phrases which frequently appear in the history of philosophy, we may say:

(1) That human beings have a "right" to personal development—that is, a "right" to realize the highest aspects of their natures.

(2) That such realization is to be found in the pursuit of certain ends or goals which have value.

[1] See Chapter 5, pp. 116–118.   [2] See Chapter 3, pp. 63, 64.

[3] See Chapter 5, pp. 117, 118.

(3) That it is the business of society to guarantee this "right".

An examination of the notion of "rights" leads us, then, by a roundabout route, back to the ethical question we have already raised—namely, what are the ideal ends in the pursuit of which the highest aspects of our nature are realized.

3. The True Ends of Politics

Recapitulation

We have seen that in order to find a basis for the so-called "rights" of the individual, we must look not to the origin from which society may be supposed to have taken its rise, but to the ends or goals which its members must, if they are to realize their natures, pursue, "rights", to put it more technically, must be interpreted not by reference to origins, but by reference to ends or goals; [1] these ends or goals, we have further seen, are fully realizable only by those who have reached the highest development of which their natures are capable. If we say that these ends are "natural" to man, we mean "natural" only for those who have fully realized the latent potentialities of human nature. And we have further qualified the statement that man must develop the potentialities of his nature with the proviso that only the highest and best should be so developed. A man, then, has a "right" to the development of the highest and best potentialities of his nature in pursuit of certain ends or goals. Finally, we have seen that this "right" can be guaranteed to him only in a society. If we add that a man has also a right to happiness, we reach the conclusion that the object of political action is to promote both the happiness and the development of the highest elements in the personality of citizens; that these, in fact, are the purposes of the State.

Distinctions between the End which is Happiness and the End which is the Development of Personality

At this point a distinction must be made between the right to happiness and the right to the development of the highest

[1] See Chapter 5, pp. 116–118, for an account of the significance of this opposition.

elements of personality, which I have hitherto treated as if they were on all fours. It is a double distinction.

(a) The first distinction is that the happiness of citizens can be directly promoted by the State. Some philosophers, the utilitarians, have maintained that the sole criterion of State action was the extent to which it promoted the happiness of citizens. "Morality," said Bentham, "is the art of directing men's actions to the production of the greatest quantity of happiness on the part of those whose interest is in view." And he went on to state what he calls the "principle of utility" as, "that principle which approves or disapproves of every action whatsoever, according to the tendency which it appears to have to augment or diminish the happiness of the party whose interest is in question."

Bentham's, no doubt, is a good common sense test but unless we believe, as Bentham did, that pleasure is the sole good or value, [1] we cannot accept it as the sole test by which to judge the merits of political legislation. Nevertheless, there can be no doubt that the State can, by the actions it takes, the training it gives, the laws it passes and the institutions it sets up, definitely augment or diminish the happiness of its citizens. Thus, such institutions as the Star Chamber, the slave compound, and the Concentration Camp, obviously make against happiness, whereas legislation designed to give effect to the provisions of the Beveridge Report [2] would almost certainly increase it, though in this sphere, the sphere of social legislation, it is the diminution of the causes of unhappiness rather than the direct promotion of happiness that is chiefly involved. [3]

When, however, we consider the case of personality, it is the removal of hindrances to development in the shape of want, fear, ignorance, injustice and oppression, rather than the positive promotion and direction of development that the State can most appropriately undertake. The State, no doubt, can provide education, and education develops the minds of those who benefit from it, but in all matters pertaining to the individual soul, to its progress in the direction of seeing

[1] See Chapter 5, pp. 133–136, for a reference to this view.

[2] A report prepared for the British Government in 1942 proposing social security legislation "from the cradle to the grave" for all British citizens.

[3] See the argument on pp. 152–155, above.

more beauty in the world, of caring more for truth, of developing a more sensitive conscience, a keener feeling for right, a more intense appreciation of good, and of achieving a higher standard of personal relations, it is doubtful whether State action can do more than remove material and social hindrances. A man's good is something which in the last resort he alone can pursue, for a man's good is individual and establishes itself for different men under different forms. In all matters pertaining to the soul of man we have come to realize that individual insight and initiative are of primary importance—have not all advances in morality been due to the moral "eccentricity" of individual men and women?—and should not be cramped or even interfered with by the State. The creation of beauty, the development of good taste in its appreciation, the deliverances of conscience and the integrity of the moral judgment, the respect for and pursuit of truth, the understanding and development of personality and of the relations between personalities—all these are matters outside the scope of State action. The State can clear the decks, so that its citizens should be free to pursue these goods, but, having done so, must leave the stage to the individual soul upon which the drama of the good life must be played out.

The Development of Human Faculty as a Prerequisite of the Good Life

(b) The second distinction is this: when we are asked to say why happiness is a good, we can give no answer to the question,[1] for happiness, being an ultimate value, is not desired for the sake of anything else, and, as we have already seen, any reasons which can be given for thinking something to be good or valuable, take the form of specifying some other thing for the sake of which it is desired; but if the thing in question is an ultimate value, then there is no other thing for the sake of which it is desired. Thus, we can only say that the value of happiness is intuitively perceived and since, if we are right, the State can positively promote the happiness of its citizens, we may now add that the duty of the State to legislate with a view to increasing the happiness of citizens is a duty which is also intuitively perceived; at any rate if anybody questions that this *is* the State's duty, I do not see by

[1] See the argument in Chapter 5, p. 53.

means of what arguments the fact is to be established. But when we consider the other goal of State action, the provision of those conditions in which the highest potentialities of the citizen can be realized, the position is different. Whatever our conception of a full and valuable life may be, unless our faculties are trained and developed, we cannot, it is obvious, live such a life. If we are not fully developed men and women we cannot enjoy the pleasures proper to mankind; for example, if we have not refined and developed our senses of seeing and hearing by intercourse with beautiful sights and sounds, we cannot appreciate great pictures and respond to great music; if our minds have not been trained, we cannot be moved by intellectual curiosity or feel the thrill of discovery in the realms of science and philosophy, or enjoy the pleasures of intellectual intercourse; if our spirits have not been cultivated by prayer, enriched by meditation and sharpened by the constant endeavor to increase in virtue and the love of God, we cannot, so the religions tell us, fully enjoy the benefits of God's goodness and love. And if anybody chooses to think that these are high-falutin' examples, I refer him to that teaching of his own experience, which assures him that it is only in so far as he knows something about a thing that he can feel an interest in it—only in so far as he knows about machines that he enjoys being shown machines; only in so far as he has some acquaintance with farms or horses, that he enjoys being shown his friend's crops and stables; only in so far as he knows something about food and wine that he will be able to appreciate those mysteriously *recherché* dishes served to him in the little restaurants of Montparnasse. A cat can look at a chessboard, but her casual glance lacks the interest of comprehension; a wife can scan the page of symbols in which the careful calculations of her mathematical husband have been embodied, but to her they are only meaningless marks on a white background, and unless she has been well-trained, the husband will, as likely as not, find them in the waste-paper basket, or serving as the foundation of his study fire.

Our interest in things, in short, is in large measure proportionate to our knowledge, and not only our interest but our love. One of the many arguments for the reading of great literature is that by enlarging our vision and deepening our understanding of the world, it enables us to see more beauty and more passion, more scope for our sympathy and insight in life than we saw before; thus, literature makes life more interesting. We must, then, cultivate our minds with zeal because the more intelligent we are, the more interesting we shall find the world in which we are placed; we must develop the highest elements in our personality because it is only in and through them that we can apprehend and appreciate those things which are valuable, the things which we have called good in themselves. What then—and here at last we come to the crucial question—are the highest elements in our personality, and what the things which are good in themselves?

Digression on the Greeks, Ourselves and the Art of Living

As I began this book with a sketch of some of the theories of the great Greek philosophers, so it is to Greek philosophy that I turn for my answer and my ending. I make no apology for doing this. The Greeks seem to me to be like men who gave the right answers to a number of sums which their successors have been getting wrong in various ways ever since. The sums belong to the arithmetic of living, and the answers are variations on the theme of how life should be lived. Holding this view of the Greeks in general, I hold Plato and Aristotle to be the greatest of the philosophers and, as their writings have been largely responsible for forming my own attitude to philosophy, it is natural that I should turn to them for an answer to the questions, what are the highest elements in our personality and what the things which are good in themselves? The two questions are obviously closely linked since, following Aristotle, I take it for granted that the best life for man consists in the cultivation of our highest faculties in the appreciation and pursuit of those things which are good in themselves.

It is Aristotle, moreover, who insists throughout his treatment of moral and social problems that the object of studying both ethics and politics is to discover how to make people good. "Political societies," he tells us, "exist for the sake of noble actions and not merely of a common life;" to translate into the language which I have adopted throughout this chapter, it is the object of politics to establish those conditions in which the best life is possible for all citizens, the best life consisting of the development of the highest elements in our personality plus happiness.

The Moderns and the Art of Life

There is another reason why it is to the Greek thinkers, and not to our own, that I go for an answer to my question. It seems to me that the moderns know comparatively little about those ends of life in the pursuit of which excellence of living consists. How could we know much, when we spend four-fifths of our waking life in getting the means to make life possible? To the art of life, surely the most important of all the arts, we bring tired minds and jaded energies and the fag-ends of days devoted to acquiring the wherewithal to live. Consequently, when we go on holiday with freedom and leisure for living, we know so little how to use it that most of us demand nothing better at the end of our fortnight than that we should be allowed to go back to work.

When, free to live as we please, we set about practicing the art of life, our notions rotate around two concepts, the concept of the expenditure of money and the concept of the movement of matter. The concept of the expenditure of money means that we pay somebody else to do for us the entertaining that we cannot do for ourselves, and as we insert our coins in metal slots, crowd struggling through clicking turnstiles, or sit in the dark to watch photographs speaking and singing, we indirectly confess our own bankruptcy in the art of living. The concept that centers upon the movement of matter relates chiefly to our own bodies. Before the war such movement was treated as an end and was valued for its own sake. A generation grew up who thought that any place was better than the one in which it happened to be, and would accordingly move heaven and earth to save five minutes without the faintest notion of what to do with them when it had saved them.

Provided that one moved somewhere in the car, it mattered very little whither one moved and, as the countryside became increasingly invaded by a generation which, unable to create beauty for itself, could not preserve the beauty which had been bequeathed to it by a more gracious past, England was being fast transformed into a land in which the facilities for movement from place to place increased in proportion as the desirability of the places to which one moved diminished. Movement was also accounted a good in pieces of matter other than one's own body, especially if they were round, and to hit, push, smack or kick round bits of matter in the right directions, at the right speeds and at the right moments with mallets, clubs, racquets, sticks or bats, exemplified for many the concept of the good life—to do this and to watch others doing it.

The Education of the Moderns

The case of the retired business man[1] is a parable of our times which, taken in conjunction with the tendencies of which it is the logical development, affords evidence that in spite of our unprecedented mastery of means there is something amiss in our conception of the ends and purposes of life. "Surely," says the essayist Hazlitt, "life if it be not long is tedious, since we are forced to call in the assistance of so many trifles to rid us of our time." This inability to tolerate our leisure without either paying money or moving matter is in fact the result of our illiberal education, that is to say, of an education mainly devoted to securing proficiency in a particular craft, science or profession. This, precisely because it *is* a specialist education, restricts a man's outlook, giving him technical knowledge of certain things but not a general understanding of important things. It fails, therefore, to provide him with a perspective for living or a scale of values, by reference to which the worth of different kinds of activity can be measured and assessed. Such an education and the avocations to which it leads, more particularly those of the business man, the technician, the engineer, and the mechanic, inevitably set their stamp upon the personality. A "liberal" education, both Aristotle and Plato would have agreed, is one which, as the name suggests, makes a man free, free both of the cravings of the body, which demand that the senses be satisfied, and of the solicitations of the mind, which demand that it should be kept amused. Now to be in bondage to the need for action or entertainment to relieve our boredom is only one degree more tolerable than to be in servitude to the solicitations of the senses to relieve our cravings. It is significant that for both Plato and Aristotle a "gentleman" is a man of leisure, one who follows no employment; only such a one they thought could attend to the art of living and cultivate the soul. And here I return from my digression to take up my main thread, which

[1] I described it above, see p. 151.

is the answer of the Greeks to the questions, what are the highest elements in our personality and what are the things which are good in themselves?

Aristotle on the Distinguishing Characteristics of Man

Aristotle points out in his *Ethics* that the excellence or virtue of a thing is to be found in the performance of its specifically distinguishing function. Thus, the function of the eye is to see and the excellence or virtue of the eye is that it should see well; the function of a piano is to play and the excellence or virtue of a piano is to play well. Similarly, the excellence or virtue of a man will be found in the right performance of his specific functions, not, that is to say, in the life of growing, which vegetables also do, or in the life of feeding or mating, which men share with the animals, but in that kind of life which men alone can live.

What is that? Aristotle's answer is that man, alone among living creatures, possesses reason, and it is the function of reason to plan and to guide; man, in fact, can lay down rules, conceive ends and plan the means for their achievement. The good life, then, is in the first place a life that satisfies this condition; it must call into play man's specific faculties, those which man alone possesses, and it must be lived in accordance with a rule.

This does not take us very far. Can we say anything more about man's specific faculties? We can say two things: first, man is a political and social animal, he lives in society, and it is only in society, as we have seen, that he can realize all that he has it in him to be; secondly, he can use his reason disinterestedly, in scientific inquiry, in artistic activity and appreciation and in speculation and contemplation. Let us consider each of these activities separately.

A. The Good for Man, the Citizen

Aristotle never suggests that the good for man can be achieved by the individual as an individual; he thinks of it always as the good of a citizen. And this for two reasons: first, it is only by contact with his fellows that, as we have seen, man can develop his nature; secondly, if the community is badly governed he cannot realize himself either as a citizen or in any other way. It is, therefore, the business of the community so to guarantee the social background of our lives that our minds and spirits can be freed for activity in accordance with man's specific function.

(i) That man can only realize himself as a citizen is a point frequently insisted upon both by Plato and Aristotle. Consider a congenital Robinson Crusoe growing up without human intercourse, with nobody to care for and nobody to hate; with no occasion to be selfish and none to be unselfish; with no ties and no obligations; with no opportunities for cheating and dishonesty and none, therefore, for the development of truthfulness and integrity of character. As he had never been to a meeting, exchanged views, read a book, discussed, argued, even talked, his intellect would be as dormant as his moral and social senses. Is it not clear that such a one would have been deprived of his title to full humanity; that he would be a man aborted?

How Far and in what Sense Force is Necessary in a Society

(ii) Secondly, though it is true that society is necessary to the development of human nature, a man cannot fully develop his nature, cannot, therefore, come to his full stature in an unjust or oppressive society. He cannot do so, for example, in the slave compound or in the Concentration Camp; he cannot, I would venture to add, in a totalitarian State, where he is denied freedom to speak, freedom to hear, freedom to write, to read and to think.

Take, for instance, the question of fear. It was maintained by, for example, the upholders of some forms of the Social Contract theory[1] of the origin of society that man lives in society unwillingly and obeys its laws only through fear. If man lived in society willingly, they argued, it would not be necessary to establish, as every society has established, a system of law, and to back its decisions with the police force and the prisons. Why force people to do what they naturally want to do? This view is put with great vividness in the speeches of Glaucon and Adeimantus at the beginning of the second book of Plato's *Republic*.

The answer to it consists in pointing out that force is neces-

[1] See pp. 157, 158, above.

sary in a society, not because most people obey the laws unwillingly, through fear of the consequences if they break them and are found out, but because of the presence in every society of a few unrepresentative and anti-social individuals whose activities, if unchecked, would make life impossible for the rest; force, in a word, is necessary against Nature's gangsters and thugs. All high-grade activity is at the mercy of low-grade activity, which, unless it is checked, will destroy the high-grade. The philosopher cannot philosophize while his next-door neighbor is assaulting his wife; the musician cannot compose while the burglar is stealing his spoons; or the good *bourgeois* go peaceably about his business if he is in momentary fear of a gangster "hold up" in the street. The same truth holds of liberty of speech. Our generation has discovered that freedom of speech for gangsters too often means no freedom of speech for anybody except gangsters. Even writing and reading are at the mercy of noise, and the morning's work of many a sage and scholar has been ruined by the vacuum cleaner, the next-door television, the palpitations of the internal-combustion engine or the unchecked yelling of the human young. Force, then, is necessary in a society, not because most people are anti-social, but because a few are, and the anti-social activities of the few would inhibit the social activities of the many. This need for the restraint of the anti-social few affords only one example of the truth that the exercise of the most developed aspects of human personality is possible only in certain kinds of society.

The Principles which Constitute the Indispensable Background of the Good Society

In general, it may be said that the thought of the last two thousand years has resulted in a wide measure of agreement as to the principles which must be observed in any society in which the exercise of the most developed aspects of the personality of the citizens is to be possible. They are principles which, taken for granted fifty years ago, have been thrown into high relief by the melancholy events of the last twenty years. First, the individual is entitled to respect as an end in himself, with a right to happiness in this world and a chance of salvation in the next. No claim on the part of the State is entitled to override this right or to imperil this chance. For, secondly, the State is made for man, and not man for the State. Its function is to establish those conditions of order, law, security and justice, in which alone the individual can live the good life as he conceives it, develop his personality, and realize all that he has it in him to be. Thirdly, every individual has certain rights; among these are rights to liberty of action, of thought and of speech, to security from violence, to property and to health. He also has an equal right with every other citizen to such education as will fit him to make the most of his natural capacities and to render to the community such services as are appropriate to his talents. The inventions of printing and the wireless suggest the addition of a right to such information as may be available with regard to current events and to protection against lying propaganda deliberately disseminated by authority. Fourthly, the individual should have a voice in determining the nature of the society in which he lives; through his elected representatives he should help to make the laws by which he is governed, and, if he disapproves of them, and can persuade a sufficient number of his fellow-citizens to agree with him, he should be entitled to change them. Fifthly, the individual should not be arrested save for offenses prescribed by the law of the land; if arrested, he should not be held in prison without trial, and his trial should be by an independent judiciary.

All these are principles which, I would suggest, must be observed by any State that claims the title of civilized. They are the minimum safeguards of the "rights"[1] of the citizen, who may thus be said to have a "right" to their observance by the community. This "right" is, however, conditioned by the admission of a prior "right", the "right", namely, to develop the highest elements of his personality; the "right", in other words, to live the good life.

So much having been premised as to the minimum social and political background of the good life, I return to the consideration of its positive content.

The Life of the Statesman

It was the fact that man is first and foremost a citizen that led Aristotle to regard the art of the statesman as the highest art.[2] What is more, he often writes as if the life of the statesman were the highest kind of life. For if the production of

<hr>

[1] See p. 144, above, for the technical use of this word.
[2] See p. 157, above

goodness in ourselves depends upon the establishment of a right social background and right social relations, and if the establishment of right social relations is the business of the statesman, then the proper performance of the statesman's function is the condition of the achievement by all citizens of such goodness as belongs to their natures. Now this we have seen to consist in the exercise of the highest aspects of their personalities. The statesman must, then, know what are the highest aspects of human personality and in what their exercise consists—must, in fact, know what is the best life for man, if he is so to frame the laws of society that all citizens will have the opportunity of living it.

Can we follow Aristotle in assigning to the statesman the highest kind of human life? I think not, and for two reasons, to the second of which he himself, in other parts of his writings, subscribes.

Aristotle agrees with Plato[1] that it is the business of the statesman to prescribe the good life for the citizens, and so to educate and train them that they will automatically tend to live it. It is because it is the statesman's business to prescribe to the practitioners of all the other professions—the educator, the lawyer, the economist, the producer, whether employer or employee—the kind of life which they must live if their activities are to conduce to the end of the general well-being of the community, that Aristotle called the statesman's the supreme art. It is implied that there is only a limited number of good lives—Plato, as we have seen, maintained that there were three[2]—that the statesman knows what they are, and that by education and legislation he can promote them. Largely as a result of the teaching of Christianity, most of those who belong to the modern democratic world of the West, have, I think, ceased to hold this view.

The Influence of Christianity

The political thought of the West derives from two sources, one Greek, the other Christian. Christianity taught that man is not only a citizen, but is also an immortal soul made in the image of his Creator; it taught, further, that his sojourn in the flesh upon this planet is temporary, and that this world is only an ante-chamber to the mansions of true Being, existence here being a short rehearsal for real existence hereafter.

[1] See Chapter 3, pp. 63–66.   [2] See Chapter 3, pp. 56–59.

Nothing, then, that happens to man, the citizen, is of comparable importance to what happens to man, the son of God who is an immortal soul. (The first of the five principles stated above[1] is, it is obvious, of Christian, rather than of Greek, origin.) This being so, the State would clearly be exceeding its function, if it were to seek to prescribe the nature of the true good for the individual. Provided that he lives the life of the good citizen—provided, that is to say, that he serves the community and keeps the laws—then, according to Christianity, he has a "right" to choose his "good" for himself. Now the life of the good citizen is not in a modern State a very exacting life. In peace-time he kept the laws, paid his taxes, served as a juror and voted. Did being a good citizen involve, in peace-time, very much more than that? Not for most of us, though perhaps it ought to have done. Moral development, the appreciation of art and beauty, the refinement of the spiritual consciousness, the perception and observance of the finer points of personal relationship, even the making of money—all these things, so at least the democratic tradition runs, are the concern of the individual and not of the State. When the State aspires to interfere in private affairs, as it does under the totalitarian *régimes,* our instinctive reaction is to regard its interference as an impertinence. "I don't want any Gestapo official prying into my private life"—such, I take it, would be the normal protest of the normal Englishman, and the set of values which it implies is, as I have said, Christian rather than Greek.

The Genius and the Community

Christianity has been responsible for a further modification of the Greek view. It has laid great stress on the importance of individual insight. The voice of conscience, it has said, is the voice of God, and the voice of conscience may speak through the most unlikely individuals; when it does so speak, the State interferes at its peril. No Greek could have understood, still less permitted, the phenomenon of the conscientious objector. We have been sufficiently impregnated with the Christian thought to admit his claim in theory, even while we constantly deny it in practice.

[1] See above, p. 168.

No doubt this claim by the individual to follow the voice of his conscience, or even of his Church, has its dangers: if pressed too far it results in anarchy. Nevertheless, it is a fact that all advances in moral insight—one thinks here of Socrates, of Christ, of Bunyan, of Tolstoy, of Ibsen or of Shaw—like all advances in aesthetic perception—one thinks of Giotto, Cézanne, Picasso, Bach, Beethoven, Wagner—have been due not to the wisdom of States or statesmen but to the original genius of individuals. The community may secure and stabilize the life of mankind; but it is to the individual that man owes his development.

That all advances in moral, political and aesthetic insight are due to the exceptionally gifted individual would be now fairly generally conceded by the citizens of most democratic communities. As a corollary, we demand that the individual should be free to follow the light as he sees it. We realize, of course, that in morals, in politics, in aesthetics, and in the realm of the spirit the light may lead him into what seem to us to be strange paths and it is always possible that he may be following a light that is not there. Worse still, we must concede that we may not be able to tell at the time whether it is the light of genius or a will o' the wisp that leads him. In other words, the originally gifted man is bound to shock his contemporaries, nor will they be able to distinguish the oddity in which his "shockingness" consists from the eccentricity of the madman and the fool. Most perplexing of all, the same man may be compact of all three, playing the genius, the madman and the fool successively and sometimes even simultaneously. Knowing all these things, and as citizens of a civilized democracy, the inheritors of a century and a half of liberal thinking, we ought to know them, remembering, too, that each individual is an immortal soul and that however weak, foolish and sinful he may be, he is, nevertheless, in the eyes of God the equal of the highest and wisest and, if only for that reason, deserving of respect, we shall conclude that every man is free to live the good life as he sees it, that, as individuals vary there may be, indeed there are, many different kinds of good life, and we shall refuse to follow Plato and Aristotle in holding that there are at most two or three different kinds of good life which it is the business of the statesmen to prescribe for the citizens. Finally, always excepting the value of happiness, which, we have already conceded, it is the business of the State directly to promote, we shall not regard the positive promotion of the moral good of its citizens as falling within its function. Provided that the State removes hindrances to the full development of the personality of citizens, we are prepared to concede that it is doing all that can be expected of it. The art of the statesman cannot, then, be for us, as it would seem to have been for Aristotle, the highest of all the arts or its excellence the greatest of human excellences.

B. The Good for Man, the Individual

Nor, indeed, was it in the last resort for Aristotle. In the last resort he admits there is an excellence beyond the excellence of the statesman, and that man has ends which lie outside the purview of the State. Political activity, he agrees with Plato, is never an end in itself, should never, that is to say, be pursued solely for its own sake, but in order to win leisure and to ensure the worthy and noble employment of that leisure. Just as the return of Plato's Guardians to the Cave to govern the State was conceived as a social and political obligation, their true good being found in the contemplation of reality,[1] so, too, in Aristotle's view, the highest good for man is the right employment of his faculties in the contemplation and pursuit of appropriate ends. Thus, the life of the statesman is, in the last resort, only a means to another life, the life that consists in the cultivation of the highest faculties of the individual in the pursuit of ends that are good in themselves. The proper regulation of the affairs of the State is, then, important mainly because, as we have seen above, a man cannot live the highest life, if he is fearful or insecure or oppressed. Thus the State is in the last resort for Aristotle too, a remover of hindrances to the right conduct of the individual's life and the development of the highest elements in his personality. And so, at last, we come to the question, in what does the development of the highest elements in our personality consist? Or, more simply, in what does the best life for man consist?

[1] See Chapter 3, pp. 61–62.

The Nature of the Good Life

In the course of the preceding discussion we have accumulated a good deal of material for our answer. Let me summarize this material:

(1) The good life is not to be found in the cultivation and pursuit of the ends which most men have actually pursued, both now and in the past; not, then, in the pursuit of money. I have known three millionaires in my life, but none of them, it was obvious, was living the good life for man; they were boring men, uneducated and domineering. Nor in that of power; I have never actually known a dictator,[1] but a slight acquaintance with the history of mankind makes it abundantly apparent that none of those great swelling figures that strut, vaunting themselves, up and down the pages of the history books—the Caliphs, Sultans, Emperors, Kings, dictators—was living the good life for man: they have been capricious and self-indulgent; they have lived in servitude to their desires and in fear of their peoples, and they have used their power to organize the mass slaughter and misery of their fellows. Nor in speed; for this modern good, as I have tried to show, is good as a means rather than as an end. It is of little use to increase man's ability rapidly to alter the position of matter in space, if he does not know what to do with it or with himself, when he has moved it.

(2) I have tried to establish a second conclusion: namely, that most of the goods that statesmen pursue are like speed —good as means rather than as ends: social security, freedom from want, good health and housing, even liberty and education are means to fuller and better living; or, as I prefer to put it, they set men free for fuller and better living.

(3) There is a sense in which men may be said to have a "right" to fuller and better living, not because when they enter society they bring with them a string of rights which derive from a presocial condition, but because each man has a right to develop the highest elements of his personality in the pursuit of ends which are good in themselves.

(4) It is the function of the State to help him to do so. This function it performs not directly, since it is not the

[1] I did, though, once have tea with one of them, albeit a little one.

business of the statesman to prescribe the good life for the individual, but indirectly, through the provision of a favorable background and the removal of hindrances. It is the purpose of politics, in other words, to establish the conditions, physical, (health, housing and employment), mental, (a good education) and moral and spiritual, (freedom of religious worship and access to what great men have thought and said memorably about life), in which the development of the highest and best elements of the personalities of the citizens is alone possible. There is also a positive good or value, happiness, which the State should seek to increase mainly through the elimination of the social causes of unhappiness.

(5) The highest elements of our personality are those which are distinctive of man and are not shared by him with the animals and plants.

We can now proceed to suggest an answer to the question, wherein is the development of the highest elements of our personality to be found?

Ends which are Good in Themselves

In view of the preceding discussions and, more particularly, those in Chapters 3 and 5, the answer should be clear. The highest elements in our personality are developed by the pursuit and the cultivation of those things which are good in themselves. What are they? Broadly, the answer which mankind has given to this question is that they are happiness, moral goodness, beauty and truth. If we ask why these things are good in themselves, no answer can, as we have seen, be given, since if things are ultimately valuable, no reason can be adduced why they are valuable; we can only call in witness the testimony of humanity which, broadly speaking, has in all ages pronounced them to be so. Listen, for example, to Hazlitt: "the contemplation of truth and beauty is the proper object for which we were created which calls forth the most intense desires of the soul and of which it never tires."

To these we must add the moral worth of the man who endeavors to increase in respect of goodness, taking care to point out that in spite of the numerous varieties of moral code and religious creed:

(i) we can most of us recognize a good man when we see one, and

(ii) the affirmations of all the world's great religions, however they may differ in their more primitive stages, tend, as the religions develop, to coincide in regard to the nature of moral good. The good man, all the religions have held, is merciful, not self-centered, kindly, compassionate, tolerant, just.

Now, I would suggest that if we associate these four abiding sources of value—happiness, the true, the beautiful and the good—and ask ourselves who have been the real benefactors of mankind, we shall find them among those who have with conspicuous success pursued them. For the benefactors of mankind have not been its rulers and statesmen, most of whom have thriven upon the slaughter and oppression of those whom they have ruled; nor, even, its scientific inventors —the originators, for example, of the fire, the wheel and the internal-combustion engine—who have provided men with means to fuller living, means which they have consistently misused, but the thinkers, poets, musicians, artists and saints. Of these we can say that they have both excelled in themselves and have appealed in others to what is distinctive in man—namely, his reason and his spirit. Fighting, feeding, making love, acquiring, possessing, hoarding, developing his body and the virtues of the body such as toughness and endurance, cultivating the qualities which have survival value such as fortitude, fleetness, fertility or guile, man is doing those things which the animals do as well if not better than he. Loyalty, discipline, uniformity? Ants run the corporate state better than any Fascist. Strength and ferocity? The lion beats us every time. Patience, grace and fleetness? In patience the tortoise, in grace and fleetness, the deer, are our undeniable superiors; nightingales are more musical, rabbits more fertile, sheep more gentle. If we value ourselves by any of these criteria, we cannot but hold that we are inferior to many of the animals. By what, then, are we distinguished from them? The answer is by virtue of our reasons and our spirits, and it is, therefore, to those who have led us in our evolutionary journey through the vast epoch of man's past in thinking, in appreciating beauty and in achieving goodness, that we owe the advance of our species beyond the animals. They are the true leaders of mankind and it was their vision and pursuit of what is true, good and beautiful which distinguished their lives and placed posterity in their debt.

Chapter 7

PRACTICAL COROLLARIES

1. Guidance

HAVING said so much on the subject of value in the preceding chapters of this book, I feel that it is time to come to a close. I cannot, however, resist the temptation of adding what the sermonizing flavor which has pervaded the last few pages inevitably insists that I should call "a few last words", one of guidance, another of warning, and a third of tidiness.

I have said that in the last resort no reasons can be given why moral goodness, truth and beauty should be regarded as ultimate values desirable in and for themselves. This is so; but certain characteristics distinguish the activities devoted to the pursuit of the values, for which those desirous of recognizing value-pursuing, or value-appreciating states of consciousness may be on the watch. Here are three:

(a) Increase of Dividends

When we are satisfying a desire or an impulse, sooner or later we get tired, and if, when tired, we persist in trying to satisfy, we become sated and tiredness turns into disgust. This happens in two ways:

(i) You can eat only a certain amount of strawberries and cream and sugar, smoke a certain number of cigarettes; presently these things lose their flavor and their savor. You cannot even enjoy the smell of a flower for more than a certain length of time; some nerve presumably gets tired, and either there is no smell or no enjoyment. The wise man knows these things, and has learned the lesson of the gratification of the senses and the desires, which is, always to stop while you still want to go on.

(ii) As you advance in years and maturity, some of your earlier tastes fall away from you; you get beyond strawberries and cream and cigarettes; you become tired of dancing and games; even of gossip and laughter. *"Tout passe, tout casse, tout lasse,"* says the old man as he comments wearily upon the bankruptcy of a life whose entries on the credit side of pleasure have come to be outweighed by those on the debit side of tedium and pain. And bankrupt it is, if the only enjoyments to be entered on the balance sheet are those of sense and desire; for it is these that flag and lose their zest, as our senses lose their freshness. But to the enjoyments which attend the pursuit of the values these melancholy reflections do not apply. The man who cares for beauty cares for it more not less, as he grows older, and can spend more time in its pursuit, in contemplating pictures, in listening to music—and to more difficult music—and in the enjoyment of nature, before tedium is felt. The scholar, the research worker, the sage, the philosopher spend not less but more time with their books and in their laboratories, and find that their interests, instead of shrivelling at their touch, grow and spread out before them, until they come to fill the horizon of their lives. Similarly the good man who aspires to become better discovers that the moral conflict is never finished and moral goodness never achieved. For the good after which he aspires recedes continually as it is approached, so that each advance in moral insight only reveals a further stage of the journey ahead, as the man ascending a mountain only realizes the full difficulty and grandeur of the climb when, the lower slopes overpassed, the dimensions of the peak that tower above are, at last, revealed. The essential quality of the moral life demands, indeed, that one goal attained, another should take its place; nor, so far as complete realization is concerned, should we shrink from being:

> "Like plants in mines which never saw the Sun,
> But dream of him and guess where he may be."

(b) Integration

In the satisfaction of our tastes and the gratification of our desires some one part only of our personality is involved. We lust with a specifically sexual, hunger with a specifically gastronomic, appetite. Ambition, the desire for power, avarice, the desire for money, fame, the desire to be known, parental affection, the calculation of ways and means, envy, jealousy and fear, all these emotions we entertain, upon all these and many more undertakings we embark, with a part of our natures only, a part which has temporarily taken control of the rest. And, as Plato pointed out, the control may become permanent, so that we fall under the domination of a single tyrannical desire.[1] In the enjoyment and cultivation of beauty, in the pursuit of truth and in the living of the moral life, all sides of our nature are engaged, engaged and integrated. In the activities of the artist, the scholar and the good man the many contradictory elements of human nature are, so long as they persist, dove-tailed, so that he both perceives with his senses, understands with his mind, appreciates with his tastes, loves with his emotions, reverences with his spirit, and resolves with his will—resolves, it may be, to become a better man, or to work harder, or to be less self-regarding, or simply to leave the world better than he found it.

It is to this integration of all the elements of our being, to the fact that temporarily and while the experience lasts we are at rest, not divided against ourselves but single, unified wholes, that the sense of peace and tranquillity traditionally associated with the contemplation of great art, absorption in study, or the sense of a duty done, arises.

(c) Change of Personality

Now it is not to be supposed that a man can have intermittent and, if the contention in (a) is right, growing contact with reality—for nothing else is being claimed for the consciousness of value—without being himself affected thereby. Satisfy your desires, obey your impulses and, when they are done with, you are left pretty much as you were before, except in so far as "over indulged" they grow with what they feed on and become your masters.

But you cannot integrate your personality without affecting it according to the manner of your integration. If you spend your life in study and the pursuit of truth, you become a scholar. The scholar has his peculiar virtues and defects, but he is apt to be immune from the smaller temptations which make up most people's lives, to be armored against the toothaches and pimples of experience. He may even on occasion achieve the tranquillity traditionally, but usually unjustifiably, associated with the philosopher.

Woo beauty as artist, musician, film-director, photographer,

[1] See Chapter 3, p. 65.

poet, novelist or critic and you will gradually come to exhibit the characteristic virtues and vices of the artist-type. You may be unstable in character, impatient of convention and sexually irregular; you may run away with your neighbor's wife or forget to return his books. You will put things to improper uses, spreading bread and butter with the razor and cracking nuts with the curling tongs. In short, you may become what the Victorians called a Bohemian, but in doing so you will, if you are lucky, exhibit a passion for beauty, a devotion to the highest that you can conceive, and a determination to express it, which will enable you to starve in a garret in the usual way in order that you may do the work that your vision shows you for the doing, rather than earn a handsome salary by pandering to the popular taste with the artistic confectionery for which the public with its coarser concepts and less developed standards is prepared to pay.

Do your duty, help others, be compassionate and merciful, live, in fact, the Christian life, and that you are immediately recognizable for what you are—we all know a good man when we meet him, though we cannot define in what his goodness consists—the testimony of mankind bears witness.

2. Caution

The word of warning is against treating values as human products. I have already argued against such treatment in the analysis of Subjectivism in Chapter 5, but so intimately is the climate of our minds pervaded by science which recognizes only the visible and tangible as real, that it is extremely difficult for us to think of immaterial entities as possessing a reality which is independent no less of mind than of matter. For when we concede the existence of immaterial realities, our tendency is to assume that an immaterial reality must necessarily be mental; thus, we think of the values as ideals and, in so doing, contrive to slip in an implied contrast between what is ideal and what is real. Yet how can an ideal attract us, pulling us forward magnet-like to realize it, unless it exists independently of the mind which recognizes it and the efforts which are made to realize it? To suppose that an ideal which man has himself invented should have power to evoke his efforts, to fulfil his aspirations and to change his personality, is to suppose him capable of lifting himself by his own spiritual braces.

Let me, then, insist once more that ideals are values, values which are given to us and are discerned in greater or less degree by us, but that they are not the products of our own thinking.

We observe that our bodies are subject to certain laws which govern their behavior; they are the laws of dynamics and statics, the law of gravitation and the laws of growth and decay. These laws are studied and described by mathematics and by the sciences of physics, biology and physiology. The results of these studies give us, so we believe, information about the world; thus, we say, the world is so constructed that unsupported bodies fall in a vacuum with equal velocities, that the attraction between bodies in empty space varies inversely with the square of the distance between them, and that it is the nature of living organisms to be born, to grow up, to come to maturity, to grow old, to decay and to die.

In just the same way it may be the case—though we are less ready to concede it—that our minds and spirits are subject to influences and laws which belong no less than the laws of physics and mathematics to the fundamental structure of the universe. Thus, we all have a disposition to call things right and wrong, to find things ugly and beautiful and to discover what is true. The responses of the human mind to these influences which act upon it we call morality, art and knowledge. The fact that our minds are sensitive to and may be controlled by the intimations and influences that reach them from without, should teach us not less about the nature of reality than the study of the laws of chemistry and physiology which govern the growth and decay of our bodies. For just as the laws of the body give us information about the nature of the physical reality in which the body is placed, so the values which inspire our spirits and guide the development of our minds are factors in the non-physical reality in which our spiritual being is set. They are, that is to say, elements of the real world existing independently of us, no less than the laws studied by mathematics and physics.

3. Reference Back

The point of tidiness involves a reference back to button up the argument. The last chapter, in spite of its many digressions—they were in part deliberate; I wanted to show how every philosophical problem ramifies into others, one might almost say into every other philosophical problem—began as a chapter on political philosophy. What, we asked, was the object of good government, what the purpose of the good legislator, and answered that it was to produce a certain kind of community, that is to say, a community consisting of citizens living certain kinds of lives. The State, in fact, exists to promote the good life and the best State is the one whose citizens live the best lives and which actively assists them to do so either by the removal of hindrances or the promotion of happiness. We have now suggested a partial answer to the question, in what does the best life consist? It remains to extend this answer to embrace the question with which we began the last chapter, what is the kind of community which it should be the purpose of government to promote? The answer is, that it is a community of whose members a substantial and increasing proportion pursue the values in their individual lives, embody them in their standards of conduct and introduce them into the climate of taste and opinion by which the judgments of the community are formed.

More precisely, it is a community whose members value truth; who care themselves to know and care that their children should be instructed in a knowledge of it without fear of favor, without, that is to say, the prejudices of nationalism or the bias of a sectional, religious creed; who value science and scholarship and the things of the mind; who are concerned to keep their own minds alert, active and independent; who make it their business to know what is happening in the world, and in all parts of the world.

It is a community whose members value art, music and literature; who care to be surrounded by a gracious environment; who insist that their cities should be planned and spacious and their homes gracious and elegant; who maintain a high level of public and private taste and who are sensitive to beauty in all the forms of its expression and desire that its manifestations should be increased.

It is a community whose members maintain a high level of justice and fairness in their dealings one with another; who are tolerant even of individuals they dislike; who are compassionate; who have a concern for the under-dog; who do not consent to enjoy a complacent ease while others are ill-fed and ill-housed; who accept service as a public duty and are prepared to give it; who, knowing that this world is inevitably in part evil, are nevertheless determined that it shall become better by reason of the lives that they live in it.

These are some of the social expressions of the values, and it is in their increasing embodiment in the life of the community that the true object of politics is to be found.

Epilogue

ON THE VALUE OF PHILOSOPHY

I SAID at the beginning that philosophy had no effect upon life, that it did not apply to practical affairs and that it had neither message nor gospel for mankind. I said these things, exaggerating them into overstatements, to startle my readers to attention, because I feared lest students coming to philosophy for the first time might form an exaggerated notion of what it could do for them.

But now that the student has read through some part of a book on philosophy—and I hope that he has duly observed the advice given on page 13 as to the importance of skipping—I can venture to retract. First, philosophy does, I think, teach us something, though it is hard to define precisely what it teaches. But though one cannot define, one can illustrate. In the last two chapters, it endeavored to show that the job of politics is so and so and that the good State may be defined thus and thus; it told us, too, in what the highest elements of our personality consist and added that the good life is to be found in their development. In previous chapters it indicated the activities which conduce to that development and, in doing so, purported to give us some information about the nature of the world which exists independently of ourselves, telling us, for example, that it contains immaterial values which manifest themselves in and bestow some of their characteristics upon the familiar things, persons, codes, institutions and communities of the everyday world.

And these things philosophy has told us, not as religion does, apocalyptically, as, that is to say, the announcements of a truth divinely or supernaturally revealed, but without power over those who have not shared in the revelation, but as the result of a process of argument which, starting from certain principles which we all, or most of us, look upon as true, sought to elicit from them by a process of deduction the corollaries they implied, checking the results from time to time by reference to the opinions commonly held and the valuations commonly passed by ordinary men and women. The principles may be unacceptable, the chains of deduction faulty, and the conclusions incorrect—it is certainly true that many philosophers would refuse to accept them—but, while admitting this, the philosopher would add that the remedy for bad philosophy lies not in revelation, religion, science, or intuition, but in better philosophy; that is to say, in a more rigorous reasoning from principles at once more embracing and more self-evident to conclusions which are inescapably necessitated. In this sense philosophy can teach us truths, even if it has not succeeded in doing so in this book.

Now it is at this point that we are enabled to catch a glimpse of the practical effects of philosophy. Let us suppose that our analysis in Chapters 4, 5 and 6, an analysis designed to reveal certain fundamental values as realities, underlying yet manifesting themselves in the objects of the familiar world, the facts of the moral consciousness and the purposes of political action, is broadly correct. Granted this assumption, our philosophizing may be said to have issued in the conclusion that in addition to the familiar world there is another order of reality which is related to and informs the familiar world.

Such, indeed, has been the traditional teaching of the great philosophers who, however they may have differed on other matters, have with few exceptions agreed that the familiar world does not provide the principles of its own explanation, which principles must, therefore, unless the world be wholly irrational, be sought for elsewhere. This is the central teaching of philosophy, the so-called *philosophia perennis*, which, starting from Plato, runs like a continuing thread through the Scholastic philosophies of the early Middle Ages down to the present day. It is also a channel in which the streams which flow from the two sources of our civilization, Greece and Christianity, blend.

I have had much to say of the Greek presentation of this philosophy. Let me now try to put it in its Christian form. Truth, goodness, beauty and happiness are not just accidental features of reality, lying about as it were in the universe, as furniture may lie about in a forgotten room, waiting to be discovered and enjoyed; they are the ways in which an underlying unity which is almost certainly the unity of a personality has revealed Himself to man.[1] In knowing and pursuing these values we make contact, then, with an ultimate reality which is the reality of a person. But though a process of reasoning such as we have been engaged upon in this book may convince us that values exist, it cannot assist us to know them. The road to the knowledge of the values lies through experience, and to enjoy it we must embark upon a process of self-training and discipline. In morals this discipline bids us restrict ourselves to a moderate indulgence in the more obvious forms of pleasure and spurn the more superficially alluring objects of desire, that we may the more uninterruptedly pursue such things as are good, harnessing all our energies to the pursuit of a dominating purpose and resisting the thousand and one solicitations that would lead us to turn aside from it, as a man ascending a mountain may

[1] See Chapter 4, pp. 139–142.

resist the temptation to turn aside from his climb to look at the view, in the conviction that fully to enjoy its grandeur he must see it first from the top. In art it means gradually refining and enlarging our vision of beauty by a more or less continuous intercourse with the highest products of man's creative genius and a willingness to put up with a certain amount of boredom in the process of refining and cultivating our taste; for, as Sir Joshua Reynolds was careful to warn us, "it is the lowest style only of arts, whether in painting, poetry or music, that may be said in the vulgar sense to be naturally pleasing." Thus, the cultivation of a refined aesthetic as of a refined moral sense demands humility and faith. We must be humble in respect of our willingness not to condemn work which is beyond our own immediate appreciation; we must have faith in our ability to appreciate in the future what bores us in the present. Those who would pursue the value of truth are again committed to a particular attitude to life; even if they need not spurn all delights to live laborious days, they must in some degree withdraw themselves from the mass-produced pleasures of a commercial civilization.

If these things are true of a life devoted to a pursuit of the values, they are true *a fortiori* of the lives of those who would know God. Nevertheless, the general teaching of the great tradition of philosophy is that, if we live as we ought, we shall know things as they are, and that if we see things as they are, our vision will help us to live as we ought.

This is not merely a creed for the learned. It is a faith which many simple folk have embraced and by the light of which they have been willing to live. It is the faith that whoever pays the price—and it is a high one—will find the pearl. For if this, the Christian version of the traditional teaching of the philosophy of Plato, is right, if there is, indeed, a real world of values, then the faith that begins as an experiment will end as an experience.

Now whether we shall be prepared to make the initial experiment which the living of such a life requires depends, in part, upon whether we think that the existence of another order of reality is, to put it at its lowest, a plausible hypothesis. It is here that the process of philosophizing, that is to say, of close, connected logical reasoning, upon which more particularly in Chapters 4, 5 and 6 we have been engaged, becomes relevant, because, if the conclusions of our argument seem on balance to be convincing, then the faith to make the experiment upon which the living of the good life depends will seem reasonable. Here, then, is one way in which the teaching of philosophy may have practical consequences, may, in short, affect our lives.

The Philosophical Temperament

There is a further effect, the effect upon temperament. There exists a popular mythology in regard to what is called the philosophic temperament. According to this mythology, the philosopher is represented as absent-minded and inefficient in practical affairs, liable to miss trains, forget appointments and mislay his spectacles, an easy prey to the sharks and salesmen of this wicked world. In compensation, however, he is depicted as a man calm and serene, with a mind remote from the ups and downs of everyday life, able to bear life's misadventures with fortitude and to endure its tragedies with resignation. So far as my observation of contemporary philosophers goes, there is little or no evidence, at any rate among modern philosophers, to support this mythology. Philosophers, indeed, seem to be just like other men, chafed and irritable creatures with red faces, even as we are. Although, however, in any straightforward sense the myth is false, there may, nevertheless, as in the case of most myths, be substance at its root. There could not have been so much smoke blowing so continuously down the ages without a little fire. And the secret fire of the philosopher is, I suggest, precisely this belief of his that there is another world, real in a sense in which this one is ephemeral, changeless where this is changing, perfect where this is faulty. If he further believes that the real world informs and is immanent in the familiar world, and that by following a certain mode of life, by holding certain things to be valuable and cleaving to them so far as in him lies, he will increase in the knowledge and love of reality, then his belief cannot but affect the practical conduct of his life.

For if values are real they are also ideal. I do not mean by this that they are in some sense in the mind; I do mean that they are not merely objects which we can know, but goals or ends after which we should strive. For if the values are real and can be known by the human mind, then precisely because they *are* valuable, they exert a pulling power over the mind that knows them. You cannot enjoy beauty without wishing to enjoy it more fully; be good without resolving to be better; know that truth is just round the corner without wishing to track it down. Ideals, in fact, draw us forward and pull us upward, giving us a strength to rise above ourselves which without them we could not have had. Nothing can rise by virtue of its own inherent gravity and it is only in so far as the values are dynamic and—if the metaphor may be permitted —take the initiative in establishing relations with us, bidding us know them more clearly and embody them more fully in our lives, that, responding to their challenge, we shall be enabled to rise above ourselves.

Scope of Philosophical Questions

If it be objected that I am here verging on mysticism, I hasten to bring the apprehensive reader back to earth with the trite reflection that on any showing the greatness of the questions with which philosophy deals cannot but have a widening effect upon the mind that is brought into contact with them. If I may venture to repeat what I have written elsewhere,[1] "those who give time to the study of such impersonal questions are bound to preserve something of the same impartiality and freedom in the world of action and emotion. Since a consideration of fundamental questions shows us how little is certainly known, the philosopher is ready to grant that contrary views may have as much or as little truth as his own. Thus philosophy generates an attitude of tolerance which refuses to make the distinction between right and wrong, good and evil, truth and falsehood, identical with that between the things done and the views held by the self and the contrary actions and thoughts of others. Finally, the fact that no agreed answer has yet been discovered to the most fundamental questions cannot but suggest to the honest thinker that all systems hitherto constructed are in some degree false. Those who have no tincture of philosophy are inclined on all questions not susceptible of proof to supply the place of knowledge by converting other people's conjectures into dogmas. The philosopher, on the other hand, will admit that even his so-called knowledge is conjectural, and regard fanaticism, bigotry, and dogmatism not only as an offense against manners, but as a betrayal of the truth. It is for the sake of the questions which philosophy studies, and of the methods with which it pursues them, rather than for any set of answers that it propounds, that philosophy is to be valued.

"Through the greatness of the universe which it contemplates, the mind itself achieves greatness. It escapes from the circle of petty aims and desires which for most of us constitute the prison of everyday life, and forgetting the nervous little clod of wants and ailments which is the self, is elevated into communion with that which is greater than the self. On the practical side this greatness of mind generates qualities of tolerance, justice and understanding, in the growth of which lies the chief hope for the world to-day."

Topical Value of Philosophy

This attitude is particularly valuable in a time like the present, when men's minds are the prey both of insecurity and of dogma.

In an insecure age it is good to be reminded of the fact that this world is not the only one, that its prizes are not the only goods and that if our civilization finally collapses in war, something of value will yet remain. Indeed, the whole world of value would remain, while if we are right in thinking that the values both inform and inspire the familiar world, we may rest assured that civilization will again arise as a result of the effort of human minds to know, to pursue and to embody them. Moreover, a belief in the existence

[1] In *Return to Philosophy*, Chapter 8.

of the eternality of values carries with it the corollary that it is always worth while to *try*; hence it can never be right to abandon hope. Such a conviction brings comfort to men, as Christianity brought them comfort at the time of the break up of the Roman Empire.

In a dogmatic age, when men are given to the intolerant assertion of moral, economic and political doctrines, it is a welcome relief, to put it no higher, to pass into a realm of intellectual discussion in which men's reasons are not the slaves of their passions, and in which they can address themselves to the business of discovering what is the case without being distracted by the fear that their views may be pronounced wicked or degrading or pessimistic or liable to spread cosmic "alarm and despondency". Thus, philosophy provides men less with a faith by which to live than with a scale of values to regulate their living. These values can, as I have tried to show, serve not only as ideals to guide the individual's life, but as ends to direct the actions of communities, thus providing the citizen with a goal for political effort and a test by which to measure the worth of political programs and policies.

Purpose of the Book

A word, finally, about the purpose of this book. It began as a guide to philosophical reading and study for those who are embarking upon the subject for the first time; but it has outranged its original purpose and become both an exercise in philosophy and an apology for its pursuit. I have long felt that philosophy has a contribution to make, however modest, to the alleviation of the distresses of our times, and have on occasion ventured to indicate what this contribution should be.

In Plato's *Republic* Socrates says that it is only when philosophers become kings that mankind will achieve salvation. But "Look at the philosophers," say his critics, "what a sorry figure they cut in society! With what effrontery can you ask us to suppose that such men should exercise rule in the State?"

Socrates replies by the metaphor of a man taking shelter from a hailstorm under a wall. When the community is swept by gusts of partisan passion, when the hail of violent controversy is rattling about one's ears, the wise man knows that "he is not strong enough to hold out alone where all are savages. He would lose his life before he could do any benefit to the city or his friends, and so be equally useless to himself and to the world. Weighing all these considerations he holds his peace and does his own work, like a man in a storm sheltering under a wall from the driving wind of dust and hail."

Socrates's answer is, one suspects, an apology rather than a justification, for both he and Plato believed so strongly in the practical value of philosophy that they devoted a large part of their lives to the endeavor to implant its principles in the daily life of men and cities. Socrates brought philosophy down from the clouds into the market-place, and went hither and thither among the people teaching and discoursing with young men on the right life for man and the right governance of cities. Plato devoted two of his Dialogues, the *Republic* and the *Laws,* to the principles of government, and acted as tutor to the son of a ruler destined himself to hold absolute rule. Indeed, Plato's insistence upon the philosopher's duty of taking part in practical affairs led him on two occasions into serious danger of his life. In a time not very different from that of Plato, philosophers ought, in my view, to accept a similar obligation. Philosophy in the modern world has become a specialized study, divorced from life and devoted to the discussion of purely technical problems. I do not wish to suggest that this is not the business of philosophers; I say merely that it is not their whole business and that to proceed as if it were is to betray a trust. If modern philosophers have no wisdom of their own to offer to a distracted generation, they can at least seek to interpret for it, in language that it can understand, the wisdom of the great philosophies of the past. For they, after all, are the modern repositories and interpreters of that wisdom, and if they do not make it plain, nobody else will. It is in the spirit of this obligation that I have ventured to write this book.

BOOKS BY THE SAME AUTHOR

Guide to Philosophy.
Guide to the Philosophy of Morals and Politics.
Return to Philosophy.
Philosophy of Our Times.
Guide to Modern Thought.
Matter, Life and Value.
Philosophical Aspects of Modern Science.
The Recovery of Belief.

INDEX OF NAMES AND TITLES